Ruth the Truth is one of Britain's most popular psychics. A regular columnist and psychic agony aunt for the *News of the World* and *Chat* magazine, she has an amazing success rate in helping readers solve life's most challenging questions. She is a trained psycho-sexual counsellor and she also specialises in personal development. She lives in Hamilton, Scotland, with her husband and two children. This is her first book.

She cannot promise to answer you personally, but if you would like to ask Ruth any questions about the book, please contact her on urquhartruth@hotmail.com

Ruth the Truth's
PSYCHIC
GUIDE

Ruth the Truth's PSYCHIC GUIDE

*A step-by-step
guide to developing your
psychic powers*

PIATKUS

First published in 2001 by
Judy Piatkus (Publishers) Limited
5 Windmill Street
London W1T 2JA

e-mail: info@piatkus.co.uk

*A catalogue record for this book is
available from the British Library*

ISBN 0 7499 2233 8

Text design by Zena Flax
Edited by Lizzie Hutchins

This book has been printed on paper manufactured
with respect for the environment using wood from
managed sustainable resources

Data manipulation by Phoenix Photosetting, Chatham, Kent
Printed and bound in Great Britain by
Butler & Tanner Ltd, Frome, Somerset

I dedicate this book to Jessica and Thomas, my special little people who always accept Mummy, to my long-suffering husband Ronald, for just being there, and to Anna Bruce, MBE, who never gave up her battle with cancer and taught me how important today is.

Contents

Acknowledgements

I would like to thank my family for helping me with the research, especially my mum and dad, whose knowledge has helped me on this quest.

Thank you to my sisters, Ayfer and Soraya, for putting up with a part-time sister for so long.

Also to Mr Bob Bird of the *Scottish News of the World*, who saw the magic within 'Ruth the Truth' and has always supported me, not forgetting Michelle Hather, my deputy editor at *Best* magazine, for all her hard work on my column, to my new team at *Chat* magazine and all at the national *News of the World*, in particular Gary Thompson.

To my friends Lesley, June-Anne and Kathryn, who always believed I could write a book even when I felt like giving up.

And finally a big thank you to my publishers, Piatkus, especially Judy Piatkus, Sandra Rigby and Lizzie Hutchins, for helping my dream become a reality.

Introduction

OVER SIX YEARS AGO I was asked to write a book. At the time I was not in a position to take up the offer, but always knew that one day I would want to let people know how they could develop their own special powers. Fortunately I have now been able to bring you my very first book.

We all have some psychic powers. We have to, as back when we were all living in caves and looking for food, our instincts had to help us find out what was around the corner. For years during my readings with clients I have met people with powers which have ranged from very basic to acute. I remember doing a reading for an 18-year-old girl who was training to be a nurse. Her aura was golden with turquoise, so I knew she was very psychic. When I asked her if anything seemed to be strange in her life, she just looked at me and said that at times she had visions which would later mean something. I held her hand and asked her what she saw for me. I told her to close her eyes and just listen to her breathing and the visions would come. She said, 'I see a blue car and a baby.' Six months later I bought a blue car and then had my son Thomas. That girl was definitely psychic, but she had no way of developing her skills. This book is written for all of you who want to develop whatever skills you have. It is also for anyone who is interested in anything psychic – which, after all, is most of the population.

This book is going to take you on a journey. I will start by telling you where I come from and how my psychic ability has made me the person you read about today. I will relate how my famous witchdoctor bones came to me and show you a special witchdoctor oracle I have developed for you to use. This will enable you to find answers to all those burning questions! Then I will help you to develop your own psychic gifts, using the wisdom of my grannie who helped me to develop my own gifts. A lot of people who come to me for readings are interested in developing their own skills. This book will help you do just that. Everyone wants to be loved, so I show you how to go about finding a lover, then how to keep the love from fizzling out. You will find my home-grown love recipes a real hoot! Then, after helping you to bring harmony to your relationships and establish a happy family life, I turn to your health and beauty. After all, we all want to look and feel our best, don't we? Not to mention find success and financial security. I can't promise anything, but I can show you how to try. And if you're a little tired after all that, finally I'll take the zzzzzzz out of your sleep and reveal what your dreams may be telling you.

There's lots of practical advice in the book and many examples of how to use rituals in your everyday life. However, it's very important to protect yourself before you begin any ritual, even if you're simply lighting a candle for a specific goal. In any psychic work you are attracting energy, but if you want to be sure that it's always positive, you must use a form of protection. I suggest you sit quietly in a comfortable chair and close your eyes. Then imagine pressing a switch on top of your head that activates a golden light all over your body. Your protective shield is now intact – open your eyes and begin your task.

I hope you enjoy reading my book. I loved writing it.

CHAPTER 1

My Life so Far

I WAS BORN on 21st August 1968 on a hot summer's morning. The news of the day was the Russian invasion of Czechoslovakia.

I was the first-born and my mother had a very difficult time. To this day she blames me for a pain she gets as she irons. As with the rest of my life, my birth wasn't what you would term 'normal'. In her drugged post-birth haze my mum remembers the consultant telling her she had had a caul baby. I had been born into the world covered in my amniotic sac. This was a very unusual way to be born. 'This child is special and will never drown,' the doctor said. Because of this belief, the nurses said that sailors would welcome me on their boats.

From that day my mum sensed that something was different about me – but of course in a good way. My

Scottish gran whooped with delight and said, 'This is the one who will be gifted.' Thirty-five years previously she had been told by a fortune-teller that one of her grandchildren would have a very strong gift which would take them to all the corners of the Earth to help people.

I was born into a loving family with a Scottish mum who hailed from Hamilton and a Turkish dad from Istanbul. It wasn't until a couple of years ago that I discovered the true nature of my family. My great gran on my mother's side had come over to Scotland from Ireland when she was young. She settled in the Gorbals in Glasgow with her family, leaving her past well and truly buried. It would seem she may have been from a Romany family, but we have never been able to prove this. What is certain is that my gran was very gifted and that from a young age she would have 'feelings' about things which would come true. She had a very difficult life as she fell in love with a Catholic boy and this was frowned upon in the 1920s by her staunch Protestant family. Still, her love for my grandad was so strong that she gave up everything for him. Her family disowned her and it wasn't until she had her first child that they spoke to her again.

My gran often knew things before they happened. One day she began baking bread and cakes and my mother, who was only 10 or so at the time, asked her what she was doing. My gran said she was baking for the girls. 'What girls?' Mum said. 'You know, your cousins from Australia!' My mum knew there had been no letter to say they were coming and as there was no phone, how could she know? But sure enough, a couple of hours later, with the table all set, there was a knock at the door. My mum's cousins had made a surprise visit all the way from Australia. My gran always sensed that she may have come from the Romanies, but she never had proof, only small snippets that a child remembers when young. I have no doubts how special my gran was, though, and I know that I inherited my gift from her.

On the other side of my family, my father had a very difficult early life. He was born in 1940 and, although Turkey was not involved in the Second World War, the country was still affected by it and rationing was in force. My dad was the son of an accomplished weaver and a lacemaker. They lived in a one-bedroomed stone house which had a courtyard in the middle of it. In the courtyard my dad vividly remembers a beautiful mulberry tree, which in Turkish is called *dut*. Each autumn it would yield the most beautiful fruit and the amount of fruit would show how well my grandfather's towel-making business would do. The tree was nurtured just as if it were a baby, with a specialist coming in once a year to prune it and feed it a special formula.

People would come from miles around to see my grandfather at work, weaving with wooden shuttles and looms. He was a master weaver and he would tell his young son that he owed it all to Allah. My Turkish grandmother and grandfather were both Moslems and very spiritual people. As well as making lace, my grandmother would have people visit her so she could pray for them and heal them. She would sit with the Koran on her lap and open it at a page she felt drawn to. Then, after praying for the person in front of her, she would have money placed in the holy book for her hard work.

When my dad was only six he lost his beloved father and the very next day he was taken to an orphanage with his sister, my Aunt Ayfer, as my Turkish gran could not support herself and the family on her own. My gran was housed in the same complex as my father, but in a separate part, as she was too ill with arthritis to look after him or his sister. Their lives would never be the same again.

My Turkish gran also had the gift of prophecy. In fact people would even visit her in her hospital bed for guidance. She would read coffee grounds – the Turkish equivalent of reading tea leaves – and saw that my father would move away one day and marry a lady with white skin. Of course this came true. At the age of 24 my father left Istanbul to work in Glasgow for Hilton International. He was supposed to go back home after six months, but fell in love with a quiet fair-skinned Scottish girl, my mum. They were married within six months and my dad stayed in Scotland.

Unfortunately my Turkish gran died in 1968, just before I was born. But she knew my mother would have a girl and named me Yasemin, her favourite girl's name.

I was also named Ruth after my mum's sister. My gran was a very special lady. Although I never met her on the Earth plane, I was destined to meet her four years later on the spiritual plane.

Childhood memories

My first memories are of when I was three or four years old and I was living in a high-rise flat in Knightswood in Glasgow. I remember that, because we were on the 15th floor, I could look out of the window and see the whole world, or so I thought. I would play outside in a little park which was situated just at the bottom of the flats. I would often play with around 20 children, all from the flats. When I was hungry I would just call up to my mum and she would throw me down a jam sandwich wrapped in tinfoil. I loved those days and see them as very happy. By then I had a little sister, Ayfer, two years younger, and my mum had another baby on the way. I was an independent child. At the age of five I started school and was the only who went off quite happily, leaving Mum behind. Even in the nursery I had been very confident – 'bossy', as one teacher put it!

At the age of four I had a very strange dream in which a lady was telling me she was my gran. I was confused, as she didn't look at all like my gran and spoke with a strange voice. My mother recalls, 'Ruth came running into the room to tell us that a lady had come to visit her.

She spoke to us in fluent Turkish. What she said meant something to Ruth's father and we both knew she had connected with her gran, who had been dead for four years.' My father was convinced I had spoken to his mother. I had described her to a tee.

I not only had these weird dreams in which people would talk to me but I would also sense things about anyone I met. For instance when I was six we had a new schoolteacher, as our regular one was sick. As soon as I saw her I just knew something was wrong with her. I kept seeing a car crashing at speed. In fact I got so upset that I was sent home and of course my mother was worried about me. When she made some enquiries she discovered the teacher had lost a son in a car crash. Mum was gobsmacked, to say the least.

At six my life changed as we all moved to Nottinghamshire for Dad's work. It was very rural and I remember a gypsy once coming to the door. She was insistent that my mum give her money for pegs. Mum had just told her that she didn't need them when the gypsy caught sight of me peeking out between the net curtains of the living-room. Alarmed, she told my mother I had the mark of a witch on my forehead and she ran off as fast as a gazelle. Mum looked round and laughingly said that I was better than a guard dog. I have never seen what the gypsy was talking about, as my forehead seems fine to me.

My psychic gifts could be useful in other ways. My sister Ayfer recalls that when she was only three years of age she went missing while on a seaside outing with the family and was befriended by a senile old lady. 'Before I knew it I was on a bus with the old woman. Unknown to me at the time, Ruth had been asked by a police officer where I was. She told him that she hadn't seen where I had gone but that using her special eyes she could tell him where I was. The police officer decided to go along with Ruth's game. She told him that she could see I was on the top deck of a bus with an old lady sitting beside me. She also mentioned that the bus had stopped at the end of a pier.' At that the policeman ran like the clappers to the end of the pier, where the buses stopped. Ayfer was on the top deck of a bus with the lady. The police officer's face was a picture and he asked whether he could have special eyes too, to see the bad guys.

By the time I was eight I was living back in Glasgow. Then we got word of a new house in Hamilton. So it was another school and new friends and even more bullies. What I haven't mentioned yet was that for most of my school life I was traumatised by bullies who picked on me because I was dark-skinned and had a strange name and even weirder skills. But do you know something – the bullies never beat me and they made me the strong person I am today.

My psychic abilities were growing stronger and more erratic. Over and over I had a dream that my grandfather was going to come to harm somehow. The dream was so horrific that even to this day it sends chills down my spine. It is so scary that I can't tell you it for fear it would give you nightmares too. Suffice to say that in it I see my 'pop' or grandfather dead and I wake up with a start. The fifth time I had the nightmare I came downstairs to tell my mum. She was already up and I could tell by her face that something was wrong. 'Your pop's dead,' she said. I sat down in disbelief and realised I had seen the awful thing happen before my very eyes.

After his death my pop came to visit me many times. Some of these visitations were very distressing for me, especially as I was only nine at the time. He would sometimes appear at the bottom of my bed or floating just above the bed. This really freaked me out, as you can imagine.

Even after that, though, I just thought that everyone could do what I could. It wasn't until I was 11 and at high school that I realised not everyone had the same abilities as I did. That made me feel like a freak and I became very depressed. I remember vividly Mum taking me to a psychiatrist, who just said I had an overactive imagination. On the way out I told him that his wife had been angry with him that very morning for breaking her best mug. He just looked at me and said to my mum that perhaps his comments had been short-sighted. However, there was nothing he could do for me.

My knight in shining armour was in fact always just a few steps away from me – my gran. She decided that once I was 12 she would take me under her wing and train my adventurous vibes. She hadn't wanted to intervene too early as that might have restricted my personal development. But when my schoolwork started to slide and I was getting down, she knew she had to do something. Teachers at school were already complaining that I was scaring children with my so-called visions. Once I saw a friend's gran sitting beside her in class trying to talk to her. She had passed over a month before. I told another friend that her parents would separate and they did, weeks later. The teachers got fed up with this and as it was a Catholic school they couldn't be seen to condone my weird behaviour. Gran had to act for all our sanity.

Grannie's helping hand

I would go to my gran's house on either a Friday or Sunday night, depending on which night she was going to the bingo. At the start it was all very basic. She would get me to tell her what I was seeing and how I was feeling. Then later on she would give me objects to hold so that I could tell her what my vibes told me about the object. Often these would be objects which came from people I didn't know or had no contact with. I remember my gran once gave me a large monkey wrench. As soon as I held the cold metal object I got a flash of a man being crushed under a car he had been working at only a few moments earlier. I saw that the wrench had been pushed into his shoulder by the force of the car. When I relayed all of this to Gran, she smiled broadly. 'You have got it,' she said, clasping her hands.

With Gran's help I fine-tuned my skills and when I was 15 she knew I was ready to do proper readings. It was around this time that I had one of the scariest experiences of my life. I had gone into Glasgow one busy Saturday afternoon, as I loved music and vintage clothes and would trawl all the small shops which sold these treats. It was February and I was well wrapped up for the winter chill. I entered Lewis's, a large department store, to look at the books which were on sale. A bargain box caught my eye and as I could never resist a bargain I went over to investigate. As I put my hand into the box to get a book, a gloved hand touched mine. As it did so, a chill like no other filled my body. I looked at the owner of the hand and saw a very strange-looking woman staring back at me. She had a classic black bob, tailored red coat, white skin, black eyes and red lips. She said to me, 'I know who you are and what you are. I am of an opposite force.'

Totally unnerved, I just ran for my life and sat outside the store on a bench until I had seen her leave the shop and walk away. Nothing like this has ever happened to me since and I hope it never does. My gran believed that this woman was a black witch sent to scare me off and prevent me from doing my good work. It was after this that my gran taught me the importance of psychic protection and later on I will explain to you how you can apply it to your life.

As I said before, my gran now felt that I could read for the general public, so whenever she heard of a charity event or someone who needed advice she would take me along to help. My first readings were very long, as it took time for the information to come through, but in time this improved. My gran taught me four basics I still live and work by:

1. I use my powers to help people.
2. I only ever tell them what is of use to them the day I see them.
3. I never tell them anything which will make their lives worse.
4. I thank God for the gift he has given me every single day.

These four things are what make me Ruth the Truth today.

Meeting Ronald and going to university

I met my husband when I was 16 and I started going out with him when I was 17, which was only four weeks later. I won't go over the details now, as it is all in my chapter on love, but I just knew when I met him that he was the one. My mum was worried, as she thought getting serious with Ronald would mean I would give up my ambitions of going to university. Of course this wasn't true – Ronald and I both had aspirations to further our studies. I went to Glasgow University to read microbiology and Ronald went to Paisley University to study social sciences.

I decided to study science as I hoped that it could explain how my psychic abilities worked. Of course even once I had done the degree, I still hadn't really found anyone who could explain it all to me. But I also felt that through doing science I would be able to help people by working in health research in the future.

A year into my course Ronald and I were married in a lavish ceremony. So at 19 years of age I was married and a student. Broke and homeless, we spent the first couple of years of our marriage living with my mum and dad.

At university my friends soon cottoned on to what I could do. I would be able to tell them things about themselves they had never told me, or explain to them what would happen to them in their lives very soon. Best of all, people just accepted me, not like at school where they would poke fun at me and hit me. Even lecturers got in on the act. One said that the reading I gave him was the most astounding 45 minutes of his life. As he was a lecturer in physics, I asked him whether he had an explanation for what I could do. He just shrugged his shoulders and said that it must be something to do with time. He knew I *could* do it, but sadly not *how*.

Glasgow University is very old, with the most beautiful Gothic architecture. I remember one winter's night seeing the spirit of a lamplighter floating through the area known as the Quadrangle, which is a series of arches. I enjoyed my time there, but by my third year I was getting itchy feet and decided to transfer to

Strathclyde University to finish my degree on a more practical note. Strathclyde was great too.

Even with all my studying I found that my psychic ability never diminished. It just seemed to come to the surface when I needed it – as when a friend in my class thought she was pregnant. As there were only four weeks until our finals, this was the last thing she needed. I could see no baby but a pelvic infection that she would need treatment for. Sure enough, she wasn't pregnant and on seeing her doctor was told that she would need to take antibiotics for a urinary tract infection.

I left university with an upper second class honours degree and the world at my feet. Although I had worked as a volunteer helping and counselling people since I was a teenager, I felt that I should stick to a scientific career. I decided to do a PhD in bacterial adhesion to contact lenses at Caledonian University. I enjoyed it very much, but by my third year I was missing helping people, which is what I had thought my work as a research scientist was going to consist of. As it was, the only people I clapped eyes on were colleagues who would want me to help them out with their personal problems, or even lecturers who found my gift a mind-boggling subject. I also started noticing little things called babies and I wanted one.

How 'Ruth the Truth' was born

In my third year of research a friend brought me a very unusual present – witchdoctor bones all the way from

South Africa. Later I will tell you all about these, but for now all you need to know is that they told me I was pregnant. Discovering I was pregnant was one of the most amazing experiences I have ever had. At that time I was 24 and five years married. My career hadn't gone the way I had planned and to be honest I was bored with being stuck in a lab. I also had to consider the health of the baby and working with bacteria didn't seem a good idea. I was under a great deal of pressure from my department to make a decision. Just as I was doing this, I became very ill due to the pregnancy. I had to stay in hospital, as I couldn't walk. My illness was causing me to have the equivalent of a broken pelvis. I gave up my career in science and while lying in my hospital bed, heavily pregnant, I began to plan a career in journalism.

It was a time of change. Four months before I had my baby my beloved gran died of cancer, to my great distress. Then my daughter Jessica was born on 7th May 1993, the night of a full moon, weighing in at 8lb 7oz. The birth was very difficult, but at one point my gran visited me and told me I would be fine, and I knew she would not let me down.

Sitting at home with my beautiful new baby, I realised that whatever I was going to do it had to include my psychic skills and love of people. My gran, God bless her, had always seen me writing for newspapers and magazines, but being full of the wonders of science I could never see how this would happen. I knew a lot about personal development and complementary health, though, and I knew that I could write. I wrote to the *Glasgow Evening Times* asking if they needed a freelance features writer and to my astonishment they said yes. I wrote about the healing qualities of herbal teas, then crystals and finally an A–Z of fortune-telling.

As well as doing a regular column in the newspaper I began working as a counsellor for Victim Support. This led to further counselling in such varied areas as drug addiction and abused women. I found that my psychic skills would often come into play. For example I once had a drug addict who swore blind he had been clean for weeks. I looked at him and saw that he had taken drugs some 20 minutes earlier in a bus station toilet. When I told him this, he just looked at me in disbelief.

I loved my work, but I knew that I had to help more people, so I came up with a great idea: becoming Britain's first psychic agony aunt. I had a friend who had worked with me as a Saturday girl in Littlewoods when we were students and who now worked for the *Evening Times*, and she and her then boyfriend came up with the name 'Ruth the Truth'. I love it, as it explains what I do perfectly. The 'Ruth the Truth' column was born on 13th March 1996. I loved my work and by getting vibes from readers' letters and photographs I found I was able to help people at their most difficult times. It was a great feeling.

I was now invited on to television programmes on subjects as varied as the letters I received at the paper. I even had a radio slot, which gave me instant access to my public. I was enjoying my work and even being noticed in the street, which was a funny experience. I also had enough time to have another child, Thomas, who was born in 1997. He completed my family, as with two difficult pregnancies behind me I didn't want to risk a third.

I felt I was at home at the *Evening Times*; then in the winter of 1999 I started having pangs of doubt. I just had the feeling that something was about to happen and I was uncomfortable. There had been a change of editor at the paper and although I had been told my status was secure, I didn't think it was. Then I learned that the editor had had meetings with an astrologer friend of his a couple of months earlier. At the beginning of January 2000 I was lucky enough to get a job with *Best* magazine, but I was still working for the *Evening Times* as well when the call came that I was to see the editor. As I expected, he told me I didn't fit in with his revamped paper and I left – not to drown my sorrows but to work for Britain's biggest Sunday paper, the *News of the World*! You see, as my gran always taught me, you have to stay a few steps ahead of the competition. And of course you can't keep a good girl down for too long.

Working at the *News of the World* is great, as I am helping more people through my column than I could ever have imagined. In my first week I had a letter from a lady whose son had been murdered by a group of youths. He had been walking home and unfortunately bumped into a crowd of drug-crazed youngsters. Her letter was upsetting, but I knew I could help her to come to terms with what had happened. I phoned her up and told her that her son said, 'Thank you for the ball.' When I had made contact with him on the spiritual plane he had told me of this unusual gift. Once the lady had taken a deep breath she explained that before her son's casket had been closed she had put a small football in beside him, as he was an avid player. She thanked me and was content with knowing that her only son had reached the other side safe and well.

I have had many heart-breaking letters, from mothers who have lost children to people in the depths of despair. A lady once wrote to me at *Best* as she was worried about her financial situation. Looking at my trusted mystical bones, I could see that in a period of six weeks things would improve for her. I saw a letter being sent to her through the post with very good news. Six weeks later I was informed that her husband had won a settlement for unfair dismissal and that this would help them out financially.

When I set out in this work I had no idea of the journey I would go on, but one thing's for sure – I've relished every minute of it. For the future I hope to continue to help people through my articles, to write books and to do more television, as there are so many things a psychic could do on screen given the chance.

Now that you know all about my life, you can read on to discover how to use psychic power and knowledge to help yourself in your everyday life.

CHAPTER 2

The Story of my Witchdoctor Bones

I AM VERY DIFFERENT from any other psychic you will have heard of. For a start, all the way through my life there has been documented evidence that I have special powers. Secondly, I am, as far as I am aware, the only person in Britain who uses the witchdoctor bones as part of the divination process. Not any witchdoctor bones, but a set given to me by a witchdoctor thousands of miles away. These mystical bones changed my life and now with their help I change people's lives for the better every day.

Until 1992 I had accepted that my psychic visions, dreams and predictions would always be something that came to me naturally. Though I had often wondered about the merits of the tarot or toyed with reading the tea leaves, I had never imagined that I was destined to use a unique divinatory method for the rest of my life. Still, my life never has been normal, so I was not really surprised by what was to follow.

The day that changed my life

I remember it well. It was September 1992 and my friend Anne had just returned from a six-month teaching exchange in South Africa. She came in full of beans, as always, to tell me how her trip had been. She told me that she had loved the people, especially the poor children she had helped to teach in the shantytowns. In a village near Johannesburg she had had a strange experience. 'I was walking through the village with my uncle and suddenly an old man came out from a mud hut. He thrust a leather pouch into my hands, saying it was for my opposite far away!' Her uncle insisted she take the pouch and thank the elderly man, realising that he was a witchdoctor and was highly revered in his community.

On arriving back at her uncle's home Anne gingerly opened the leather pouch with her uncle looking on, rather worried. To their amazement they saw a pile of around 35 small bones, together with some crystals and shells.

'He's given you his witchdoctor bones,' Anne's uncle said in disbelief. This was very unusual as these bones are normally passed to other witchdoctors or village shamans.

The next day Anne and her uncle returned to the

village to see the old man and try to find out why he had given her his bones. On approaching the mud hut, they saw that there was a pile of rubble inside it and around it were about 20 villagers, all crying and wailing. Anne's uncle asked what had happened and was told that the witchdoctor had died that night. Anne and her uncle went back home, quietly contemplating the full extent of what had happened.

It was on the road back that Anne realised the bones were destined for me, her opposite in height and looks and far away in Scotland. When she gave me the leather pouch I had no idea of the journey this wee bag of bones was about to take me on, but my instinct told me it was all part of the bigger jigsaw that is my life.

African wisdom

On obtaining my interesting South African gift I went on a quest to find out exactly what these bones were and what on Earth I was to do with them.

Bones have been cast to foretell the future since the dawn of mankind. The practice developed from *Homo sapiens'* delicate relationship with his environment at a time when he was totally at the mercy of the weather and freaks of nature. The patterns of nature – its rhythms, if you like – became indicators of what might happen. The wise men or witchdoctors of the tribe would use bones from their wild animals, stones from the soil and shells from the sea to look into the future, casting them on to the ground and interpreting their patterns.

It is understood that the first bones used were knucklebones, probably from sheep. These bones would be carefully prepared for ceremonies in which the witchdoctor would cast them in full view of the village. Bone casting was particularly popular amongst the tribal peoples of southern and south central Africa, but relics have been discovered in Europe and Asia so it can be assumed it was a fairly worldwide practice.

Today bone casting is still practised amongst many African tribes, from the colourful Zulus to the practical Swazis. My bones are from the Zulu tribe. The Zulus and Swazis both come from southeast Africa. The Thongas, who also practise this ancient art, are located in the Transvaal region.

The name of each bone changes depending on the tribe using it, so no set of bones is the same. The bones are said to have a direct connection to the spirit world, but the most important aspect in bone casting is the diviner. Amongst the Zulus a diviner is normally identified at birth by unique marks on the body or by a strange momentous birth – as with a caul baby like me. In other tribes, such as the Thongas, a diviner will be chosen by the current medicine man.

The training that goes with this ancient art is intensive and the person chosen will always have to go through an initiation ceremony. Normally this will involve cooking the animal which has been chosen to be used for the

Map of Africa: Witchdoctor bones are used in southeast Africa.

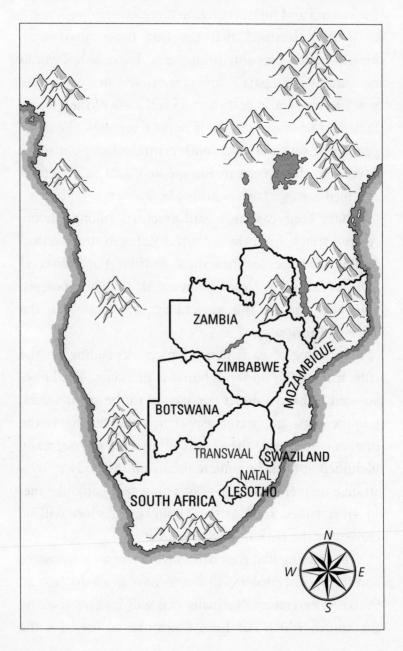

bones. The witchdoctor who will be training the apprentice will cook his bones along with the freshly killed animal. This is to ensure the new bones will bestow the same mystical powers. In most cases the apprentice will then eat the heart of the animal as a sign that the knowledge will be transferred to him from his teacher. I'm glad I had my set given to me, because as a strict vegetarian I wouldn't have fancied this process!

The trainee will go through many months of study with the bones until his mentor decides he is ready. Then at a specified date and time he will reveal his newfound knowledge to his tribe, often by doing a reading for the witchdoctor himself or another important person. If he passes this test, he will become a fully fledged witchdoctor.

My witchdoctor bones

From what I could understand, the holy man who gave my friend the bones knew that somewhere in the other side of the world there was a young psychic who could use this ancient wisdom for the good of her fellow man. After corresponding with a South African newspaper and being lucky enough to get a couple of books on the subject I quickly realised that using this mystic wisdom was my destiny.

The fact that my set not only contained bones but also crystals and shells concerned me, but I soon found out that a witchdoctor would often add to his collection to help in the fortune-telling process, so each set would reflect the diviner's personal taste. Over time I have also added to my collection.

Another thing I discovered was that when doing a reading a witchdoctor would normally draw a circle in the sand. He would divide this into segments in relation to the aspects of his client's life he would be looking at. He would then chant a holy mantra to evoke the spirits of the bones to help him in his reading and with this he would gently cast the bones. Studying them carefully, he would read their meaning and relate it to his captivated client.

When it came to using the mystical bones I sensed it would come naturally to me the first time I tried it and it also seemed surprisingly familiar to me, as if I had known all the information in a past life. I knew that the bones would work for me. After all, if a wise man in Africa thought I could do it, then who was I to deny it?

My first look at the bones

When I was given my gift what I received was a well-used brown leather pouch tied with straw. It was some weeks before I decided to open up my present. I placed all the contents on my dining-room table very carefully.

What I saw astounded and intrigued me. There were 18 small bones, 20 polished crystals and two shells. I knew right away that they were special, as the positive energy coming from them was electric. I could smell the baked soil they had been cast upon, feel the hot midday sun on my face and hear the witchdoctor chanting his mantras. With this, a man materialised in front of me. He was tall and around the age of 30. He was wearing orange and brown robes and jewellery made of shells, berries and teeth. His head-dress was like a skull cap and had feathers dangling from it. It was ornamented with colourful beads in browns and rust. He smelled awful, like a mixture of dung and urine. In fact, far from been spooked by him, I was more concerned that he would leave my dining-room smelling. He told me that his name was Sammie and that he was the spirit of my bones. He was speaking in an African language, but for some reason I knew exactly what he was saying. He explained that he would help me learn to use the bones. He asked if this was OK and when I said yes the smell went away. In its place was an exotic smell like a mixture of musk and patchouli. This was a strange but not a frightening experience.

On holding some of the bones in my hands I could sense how important they had been to the witchdoctor who had owned them, but what did they all mean? As I studied the pouch's contents I could sense Sammie's presence and then he had gone. I felt it was almost as if he agreed that the bones were now in their rightful place.

Through my research some weeks later I discovered what all of these bones meant. Each one has its own individual personality, but to help you understand how versatile they are, I have listed their most basic meanings here.

WITCHDOCTOR BONES

Ancestral Spirit 1: Decisions to be made about domestic issues.

Ancestral Spirit 2: Decisions to be made about career.

Female: If a female client is receiving a reading, this signifies her; if it is a male client, it signifies an important female in his life.

Male: If a male client is receiving a reading, this signifies him; if it is a female client, it signifies an important male in her life.

Lina: A crossroads in life.

Epok: The birth of a new idea or person/fertility.

Tanko: Employment issues. Hard work will be rewarded.

Choket: Legal matters/contracts being dealt with.

Konda: Growth, expansion.

Ceeta: Travel overseas.

Child 1: A child/childish behaviour.

Child 2: A second child/infertility problems.

Ombay: Communication on all levels.

Donga: Love affair/admirer.

Okano: Financial matters being dealt with to secure success.

Magu: Travel on the horizon.

Saury: Financial difficulties.

Aif: Good news coming.

CRYSTALS

Pink Geode: Soulmate/true love.

Amethyst Geode: You need to expand your mind/consciousness, perhaps through meditation.

Bloodstone: Physical aches and pains/need to slow down.

Ruby: Need to be perfect/a stranger has influence over you.

Botswana Agate: House move/movement in life.

Fool's Gold: Deception/may be gullible/danger.

Citrine Quartz: New beginnings.

Lapis Lazuli: Watch your back physically/emotionally.

Pink Jasper: An older person is affecting your life.

Tiger's Eye: Independence/divorce/change for the better.

Apache Tear: Luck is just around the corner.

Clear Quartz: Return to good health/positive sign for the future.

Aquamarine: Common sense will save the day.

Green Jasper: Family disharmony.

Laprodite: Overseas connections.

Rose Quartz: Healer's crystal/strong love.

Blue Lace Agate: A young girl.

Moss Agate: Contentment after a stormy period.

Moonstone: Hormone imbalance/female sensitivity.

Garnet: An important letter is on its way/change of job.

Hematite: Check out your finances.

Turtilla Agate: Your career needs to be reassessed.

Amethyst: Your well-being must be concentrated on.
Turquoise: News from overseas.
Amazonite: Education will be on the horizon.
Blue Sodalite: Circulation problems.
Obsidian: Debts.
Chrysocolla: Rewards after hard work.
Fossil Agate: Something of value is in your home.

SEASHELLS

Small Yellow: Sexual problems.
Orange/Red: Increased libido.

There you have it. My secret is finally out. You now know what my mystic bones are all about.

My next step was to put them to use.

The first time I ever used the bones

I like my Friday nights. For me they signify the end of a busy week and the start of my favourite time, the weekend. On this particular Friday night, in September 1992, my friend Anne, who had brought my bones from Africa, was coming over for wine and nibbles. I told her that I was itching to try my hand with the bones and at her request I took them down from my bedroom cupboard. I decided to cast them on the carpet, pretending that it was soil. After chanting the initiation sequence: *'I breathe on these Earth mysteries to answer my hopes and dreams'*, I threw the bones lightly on to the carpet.

The most distinctive part of what I saw before me was that the male bone was on top of the female bone and just under them, peeping out, was Child Bone 1. My husband, who had witnessed this, looked amazed as I shouted, 'I'm pregnant, I'm pregnant!' It was obvious to me what they were saying and to tell you the truth I had been trying for a baby for three months.

There was a second revelation too: the bones showed that my husband, at that time an unemployed graduate, would get a job very soon.

The next day I bought a pregnancy testing kit and indeed I was pregnant, while in the post my husband got confirmation that he had gained employment. From that moment on I knew the mystery of the bones was now part of my psychic ability.

That night I also did a reading for my friend Anne and the bones and crystals revealed that she would be getting specialist training in her job in education and that she would be happily married soon. Both came to pass within the year.

After a couple of months I decided that casting the bones and crystals on the carpet of my house wasn't very practical, especially when I had clients having to sit on the floor like Native Americans. I looked at my books again and found that, as I explained earlier, in African culture the holy man or witchdoctor would cast the bones into a circle drawn with a stick on the soil. This is called the wheel of life and is divided up into sections to represent aspects of life.

I got a piece of black material and drew a large circle on it with an acrylic pen. Then I divided the circle into eight sections. I was now going on guidance from the spirit of the African shaman who had contacted me during my first peek at the bones. With his help I had decided what would be important for my clients to know about. I divided my circle into 'Relationships', 'Home', 'Health', 'Personal Growth', 'Finances', 'Career', 'Decisions' and finally 'Surprises'. Once I had finished and the ink was dry I did another reading, this time for my mum.

The bones revealed that her health would be in question, but that she would be fine. They also hinted that there would be a positive outcome in a legal matter. Both of these events actually happened within eight weeks of the reading.

I now loved my mystical bones and with the help of Sammie, my spirit guide, I knew my next step was to use them to make a positive difference to people's lives.

Case studies using my bones

As already explained, while in hospital having my daughter Jessica I had decided that a career in science was no longer a positive option for me and had realised that helping people directly was important to my life.

When I became Britain's youngest – in fact only – psychic agony aunt at the age of 25, of course my bones came with me and the good people of Glasgow couldn't get enough of them!

I was also lucky enough at this time to start doing what I had always dreamed of – professional readings for clients. Here are some of my spookiest moments – and my blindingly accurate ones.

AN APPOINTMENT AT MY HOUSE

This lady had booked an appointment with me via an advertisement in a coffee shop. All I knew was her first name and that she would be travelling by taxi. I was in the kitchen when she came and didn't hear her knocking at the door. Luckily my husband let her in. She insisted on going immediately to the room in which the reading would take place. This was my daughter's nursery. My husband, a little uneasy at this, showed her the way. When he came down his face told me that he wasn't sure about my client.

'I don't feel right about you reading this one,' my husband said as I passed him on the stairs. I told him not to fuss and I entered the room with my bag of mystical bones in my hands.

As soon as I set eyes on the lady, a chill ran through my body. I knew that she was not the problem, but was convinced that something in her recent past was very wrong. I placed my cloth on the table and explained to her what I would be doing. I took out my bones and crystals and gave her them to cast. There is a real art to this as there are so many of them, but if you use both hands it can be done. The lady cast them on to my wheel of life and right away I could see that she had had great trouble in her career. I sensed that she worked with children and that in the line of this work she had recently shed many tears. She confirmed that this was true.

I then told her that she was a social worker, at which point a sickening image too awful even to tell you about entered my head. All I can say is that it included children being abused in the most awful way. I looked straight at her and ordered her to tell me who or what she was.

'I was a social worker on a very famous Satanic child abuse case,' she said, with tears rolling down her cheeks. 'What you have just described is what I needed to hear, as we have been told to drop the case!' She told me that I had helped her to come to terms with the depravity she had personally witnessed, but she had felt distraught when the case had collapsed and many people turned their backs on what had occurred. She believed in my gift and my bones as they had shown me so many things which were happening to her at that time. With her tape in her hand (I always record my sittings), she gave me a pile of notes and left the house in a hurry.

The money added up to well over £100, way above my charge for a reading, so I took my fee and gave the rest to a children's charity. For at least 18 months after this the images conjured up during the reading disturbed my thoughts. I couldn't do any more readings until my strength had been restored. To this day I can still see what happened as if it were yesterday.

A SURPRISE IS BROUGHT ALONG TO A READING

This time my client was a relative of an old neighbour of mine. She came along on a cold wet January morning, the type when you just want to snuggle back down in bed. She was a cheery person in her thirties and looked well on it. She had heard from her auntie how good I was and due to life changes which were about to come upon her had decided to have a reading with me.

On sitting with her I held her warm hand and felt that she had had a tough five years. I told her about the bones and she sat transfixed as I showed her what to do. When the bones had been cast I also got her to choose another crystal, as this would give me a time frame for the events which were going to unfold in front of her.

As I lifted my head up to start the reading properly I was amazed to see the figure of a little boy looking at me over the woman's shoulder. He had fair hair, brown eyes and a gap between his teeth. I would say that he was no older than 10 and with his uniform on I could tell that he was local. Of course I soon realised that he was from the spiritual plane and had a binding relationship with my client. I could see from her reading that she didn't have any children, but knew this young chap had meant a lot to her.

'Do you know a young fair-haired boy who has passed over?' I asked. 'He would be about 10 and his death was associated with water,' I added as at first she seemed a little puzzled.

Her eyes lit up and she told me that 10 years previously she had been in a local country park when she heard a commotion by the loch. On looking out to the middle of the water she saw that a boy had fallen off a boat. Automatically she had swum out to try to rescue him. Unfortunately he had died some hours later. I told her that he was grateful to her for trying to save him and that he wanted to get this message to her.

The next moment the boy said goodbye and left as quickly as he had appeared. I was happy to know that after getting this important message through he could now truly rest in peace.

I got on with the rest of the reading and the bones advised my client on a path to take in her career, which included inside information about her boss. Two months later, as foretold by my last crystal, she got her long-awaited promotion after her boss had been sacked for fiddling the accounts.

AN ANNUAL READING FOR A FRIEND

Now it is a real bane of my family's life that I don't normally do readings for them. The reason for this is that

I don't like to know what lies ahead for myself or to add to my worries about my loved ones. This rule doesn't necessarily follow with my friends, however, so some of them have annual MOT readings with me. These are basically readings to see how their lives are going and whether they can make any positive changes.

My dear friend Ruby was itching for a sitting with me so I finally found space in my diary for her between breastfeeds with Thomas and writing my column for the *Evening Times*. In her late thirties, with some difficult relationships behind her and a blossoming career, Ruby wasn't shy in letting you know that she was looking for love. She knew what she was doing and like an old pro cast her bones on to the cloth marking her wheel of life. I was so excited as I saw that in the relationship section a man was soon coming into her life and that he was from overseas.

'You've got this so wrong, Ruth. There is no way I am going to do a Shirley Valentine,' she retorted in absolute disbelief.

Unperturbed, I continued my reading, my bones also revealing that even though it was January, she would be going on holiday to a hot country by March. Again she shook her head, as she couldn't see how this would be possible. After all, it was just after Christmas and she hadn't even paid for that yet. Still, I just knew my bones were showing me that something truly exciting was going to happen, no matter how far away it seemed.

Exactly 12 weeks later Ruby phoned me up to tell me

that she was going to Morocco on holiday with a colleague from work who had won some money. More surprises were to follow, as she phoned me on getting home to let me know she had met a local man who ran a restaurant. It was love, she told me, and in the next breath she said sorry for ever doubting me.

The relationship lasted a couple of years and it proved to me yet again how accurate my mystical bones were. Funnily enough, my pal never doubted them again and she still has her annual juggle with my bones!

A READING WITH A GLASGOW UNDERWORLD BOSS!

Early on in 1999 I realised that doing readings in the house wasn't safe. This was especially true after a stalker troubled me. I opted for new premises near my home town and at first my office felt just like a second home and was great for my psychic flow.

One cold February night my mum, who was acting as my secretary, let me know that my first clients for that night had arrived. They were a husband and wife who had made it clear that during the reading no one else was allowed to enter my office and on leaving I would erase all notes of their visit. I didn't think that this was normal and neither did Mum, but I am a psychic and I do see colourful people all the time.

As soon as the couple came into my reading room, my candles blew out although there was no breeze in the office. Next one of my bones fell on to the floor, the one representing danger. Now I knew that I wasn't in danger but I did know that this guy wasn't someone I could mess about.

On beginning the reading I kept seeing the image of a gun under a bed. I also saw that children playing in the room had come across it. This played over and over in my head and I just decided to come out with it, as children's lives could be at stake and I couldn't live with that on my mind. The man said that what I had seen was very true, but because of his line of work he had to have the gun for protection. The next moment his small wife, who had just been sitting there and saying very little, got up and punched him on the nose. Then she sat down again and insisted that I continue. I quickly offered the man some tissues for his bleeding nose. The reading warned him that a gangland feud was about to turn nasty and that he should move for his family's safety. The number 15 kept coming into the equation also. The bone representing danger, which had fallen out at the beginning of the reading, was again important in the picture I saw before me.

The man assured me that he would take my advice and that the gun would be put away in a safe but accessible place. He did move to England with his family and the trouble I saw was diverted to another gangster who was found dead in the streets of Glasgow with 15 bullets in his body. The bones don't just enrich your life, they can also save it sometimes!

I hope that this has whetted your appetite on the subject of my witchdoctor bones. Next you can try out my mystic bones oracle for yourself – and there won't be a real bone in sight.

CHAPTER 3

The Witchdoctor Bones Oracle

SINCE TIME BEGAN mankind has wanted to know what the future holds. Many ancient civilisations including the Maya and the Babylonians developed oracles to help them see what the future had in store for them. An oracle is just a simple way of asking questions and getting a spontaneous answer. The ancient Chinese developed this concept further, using the *I Ching* to answer life's queries. Oracles are on the whole simple to use and can be quite a fun way of looking into the future, if not too deeply.

I have developed my very own oracle with the help of my trusty witchdoctor bones. It is a very easy system to use and will give you hours of fun. It is based on the system that I use when doing my readings. On the next page you will see the wheel of life, which is divided into six portions. Each portion deals with a specific aspect of your life. These are 'Health', 'Career and Personal

The Wheel of Life: Use this chart to look into your future.

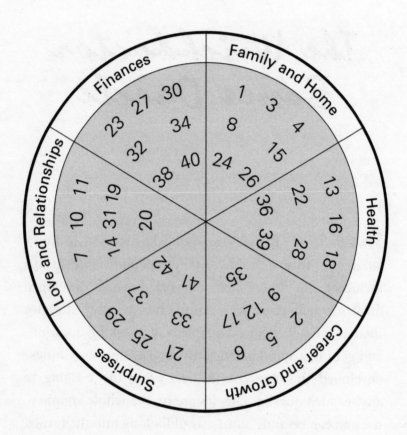

Growth', 'Surprises', 'Love and Relationships', 'Finances' and 'Family and Home'. Each section also has seven mystical numbers associated with it. These relate to the bones and crystals. Each bone and crystal has an individual meaning which will mean something to you.

HOW TO USE THE WITCHDOCTOR BONES ORACLE

Step 1: Get all distractions, such as children, partners and pets, out of the way. Make this your special time and allow yourself to be comfortable. If you are doing this with a group of friends, again take time out so that you can all get the benefits of this very special psychic tool.

Study the wheel of life and decide which aspect of your life you want to ask about. Look at it in detail, noting in your mind all the numbers you see.

Step 2: Having decided what aspect of your life you want to look at, form a question in your mind. For example it could be you decide upon 'Family and Home' and that your question is: 'How can I make my home a happy home?'

Step 3: With this question firmly in your mind, look at the relevant section, in our example 'Family and Home'. Scan once the numbers in this part, then close your eyes. Wait a couple of seconds and then open your eyes again and see which number jumps out at you. This number is your oracle number and it will answer your question.

Each number relates to a specific bone or crystal, so just look it up in the pages which follow.

For our example I chose number 1, Ancestral Spirit, which tells me that for a happy home I will need to concentrate on all aspects of home life to strike a happy balance. This is certainly true as my work sometimes impinges on my home life, as I work from home, so it is sound advice from the oracle.

Step 4: You can repeat steps 1–3 again with each new question you want to ask.

THE MEANING OF THE WITCHDOCTOR BONES AND CRYSTALS

Each bone and crystal has a mystical number associated with it. Once you have used the oracle you will know this number. You can then look it up in this section and it will give you the answer to your question.

1. *Ancestral Spirit 1:* You need to look at your domestic situation, as decisions need to be made to help this area of your life run more smoothly.
2. *Ancestral Spirit 2:* Your career is on your mind just now and it is time you were honest with yourself. Any decisions you make will be beneficial to your future.
3. *Female:* You have been putting everyone's needs before your own. It is now time to take stock and look after number one at long last.

4. **Male:** A man in your life is about to show his true intentions, so be prepared to tackle a possibly difficult situation. Let him know you have an idea of what he is doing.

5. **Lina:** Your life is coming to a crossroads. This is not an easy time for you, but handle it correctly and you will see your life improve far beyond your hopes.

6. **Epok:** You are about to reinvent yourself after a period of self-improvement. This may mean a new wardrobe or hairstyle. Whatever it is, learn to feel good about yourself.

7. **Tanko:** You have been working hard for long enough. It is about to be recognised and fairly rewarded. Bask in the glory – you deserve it.

8. **Choket:** You will be receiving a legal document very soon. Read it carefully, as you will need to sign a binding contract which could affect you and your family in the future.

9. **Konda:** Assess your life and make sure you are ready to tackle expansion. This will give you all your desires, but be ready first.

10. **Ceeta:** You are going to travel overseas to see a loved one whom you haven't seen in a while. Make sure you take a gift for the little ones.

11. **Child 1:** Someone around you is acting childishly. It is now time to let them know you are not playing along any more.

12. **Child 2:** Issues surrounding children are going to be important to you very soon. Whatever the problem,

just remember that things will get better in time.

13. **Ombay:** You are not feeling your normal bubbly self. You need to talk to someone about how you feel, as this will make things easier to sort out.

14. **Donga:** Soon you could be entering a relationship with someone who has admired you from a distance. Just try and connect to the situation and make sure that this is the right thing for you to do.

15. **Pink Geode:** Do you realise how lucky you are, as in your life there is a real soulmate who will make you happy for the rest of your life. This is a time to really enjoy yourself.

16. **Amethyst Geode:** Life has been hectic for you and you are juggling too many things. Meditation and learning to breathe properly will help a great deal.

17. **Bloodstone:** Physically you are feeling sore, with aches and pains. Improve your diet to help relieve your symptoms and look at your job, which is making things worse.

18. **Ruby:** Someone is exerting a very negative influence on you and it could be affecting your health. Don't allow this to continue. Get help from your family in this matter.

19. **Botswana Agate:** Over the next year you will have a new set of keys for a property. This will be due to a change in your relationship and it is positive.

20. **Fool's Gold:** You may have been deceived in a relationship. If this is true, do not be gullible and take decisive action, as this will be best all round.

21. **Citrine Quartz:** Out of the blue you will have to change your normal routine and a new beginning will take its place. This change is a blessing and should be welcomed, as it heralds a whole new phase in your life.

22. **Lapis Lazuli:** Is your back sore? If so, then you must do something to relieve the problem. If not, then you must be careful of what you do with your back.

23. **Pink Jasper:** An older person in your life will help you out financially, but be careful of what you must do in return. Remember there is no such thing as a free lunch.

24. **Tiger's Eye:** You are craving independence. Taking time to be by yourself and think should help. If it doesn't, then a decision to go your own way may be the solution.

25. **Apache Tear:** What a great crystal to pick. This shows that you are just entering a lucky streak in your life and that you may be hearing your name on a winners' list very soon.

26. **Clear Quartz:** Family matters will return to normal after a relative gets over a long illness through successful medical care.

27. **Aquamarine:** Use common sense where your financial problems are concerned and you will discover a way out of your problems which will keep everyone happy.

28. **Green Jasper:** Family problems lie heavy in your heart and it is affecting your health. You have done

what you could, so take a back seat now and look after number one.

29. **Rose Quartz:** Look at your hands. These are healing hands which can help people feel better just by touch. You may take this a step further by learning about Reiki, as you have a gift but you don't know it.

30. **Okano Bone:** You will soon be signing financial contracts which will bring you happiness and great success. Make sure you read all the small print, as it may be significant in the future.

31. **Magu Bone:** You will soon be given the opportunity to travel away from home for pleasure. Don't miss out on this chance as you could meet someone who changes your life forever.

32. **Saury Bone:** Your finances have not been great over the past 12–18 months. It is time to take a step back and look at your financial situation as a whole. Then there should be an improvement.

33. **Aif Bone:** Soon you will be getting good news from the postman. Just remember who your friends are.

34. **Hematite Crystal:** Study your finances now rather than later and make any changes which are required to put them on the right path again.

35. **Turtilla Agate:** A job you once only ever dreamed of could be yours. Believe in your abilities and things will go your way.

36. **Amethyst:** Your life has been hectic recently and you haven't had a minute to yourself. Emotionally you

have been on a roller-coaster and it could be beginning to affect your health.

37. **Turquoise:** You will soon be hearing from someone significant from overseas.

38. **Amazonite:** If you want the chance to increase your earnings in the future, then training and self-development will allow this to happen.

39. **Blue Sodalite:** Someone close to you has a circulation problem which will need medical attention.

40. **Obsidian:** You are starting to worry about your debts and can see no way out. Seek financial advice from an outside source and you will get a clearer picture.

41. **Chrysocolla:** You will be over the moon to hear of a close friend's success when they gain an accolade for hard work.

42. **Fossil Agate:** You don't realise it, but in your home you have a family heirloom which is worth a lot of money.

There you have it – my unique oracle to help you discover what lies ahead for you.

CHAPTER 4

Unlocking your Psychic Potential

AS I HAVE EXPLAINED, until the age of 11 I truly believed that everyone could see dead people and visions at any time, just as I could. It wasn't until I got to high school that I realised this just wasn't the case. I do feel, though, that we all have psychic potential. It is inherent within us. In earlier times we needed it to keep us ahead of our predators and to this day it is a hidden ability for most of us. My own psychic ability is very advanced and I know that it is a gift from God. That is why I only ever use it to bring about positive changes and I never take it for granted.

A normal day for me can consist of anything up to 20 'psychic pops', as I call them. This will normally mean that by the time I have dropped the kids off at school and nursery I will have had one vision or even a dead relative of the guy ahead of me at the traffic lights waving at me.

The only way I can describe my visions is that I have a kind of video recorder in the centre of my forehead. I see pictures which invariably mean something is about to happen. For example six weeks before the Concorde crash in France I was shopping for food when I saw the image of a long thin plane with flames at its back end. Later I dreamed of it as well. I do have dreams that come true, such as the one I had about my friend getting a new job she hadn't even applied for yet! Then there are the people who have passed over. I have seen them since I was a child. If you have seen the movie *Sixth Sense* then you will know just what I mean. By the time I was six I had several 'imaginary friends' who were really family and friends who had passed over and liked to communicate with me. My parents and doctor just thought that I had a very creative imagination.

You too have probably had a psychic experience, only you didn't see it that way. Say that you have just been told you are about to lose your job and are feeling upset. On the drive home you stop off at a garage for petrol and meet a friend who tells you about an opening at his workplace. Or you lose a piece of jewellery which is very dear to you and yet you find it some time later on a path to your home. Have you ever put the radio on and found that the song you are humming to yourself is playing? These are all simple examples of psychic ability, but you probably just thought that it was all coincidence.

Young children and animals have strong psychic ability. Just look at a cat on a stormy day. Well before the rain starts it will be crying to come inside. I get countless letters from worried parents whose three-year-old is pointing to a space in the corner of the room and talking and smiling as if they are speaking to a friend. Children just seem to ooze psychic energy, but for most it diminishes once they go to school. The reason for this has never been fully understood, but I think that it is mainly to do with the fact that they don't want to feel different from all the others, or that in fact they just grow out of it.

What is psychic ability?

'Psychic ability' is an umbrella heading for all subjects relating to the use of our special senses. It can be found in many forms, such as intuition, which is using our gut feelings to help us in everyday life, telepathy, which is reading others' minds, or clairvoyance, which is seeing visions or having dreams which are guides to future events.

Being from a scientific background I always like to look at things logically. Psychic ability is driven by energy and as we know there are many forms of energy – electrical, tidal, spiritual, and so on. Psychic energy, this 'special energy' as I will call it, manifests in the psychic pops I get or the meaningful dreams you may have. Just because we don't see it doesn't mean that it isn't there. To harness this energy you need to look after it and nurture it. You do this by learning to relax and concentrate on the here and now. This means no worrying about the kids or what you have to make for tea that night! Later on I will show you how to do this.

Over the 15 years that I have been doing readings I have tried to understand what I do and how I do it. The best explanation I have received was given to me by a friend of mine who was studying astrophysics when I was at university. He told me that I had the ability to see things from a different perspective. For example if trains were leaving Glasgow Queen Street station and Waverley station in Edinburgh at the same time and I had a bird's eye view from the top of a hill in Falkirk, which falls between the two stations, I would be able to see that they would crash and would have time to do something about it. It is this special viewpoint that I want to help you to develop.

How you can develop your psychic ability

Just as a top-class athlete would keep fit with a highly planned diet and fitness regime, I too have to keep my abilities highly tuned. The following is my development plan. You can follow it as well. To begin with, just take your time reading it. Get a hot drink and kick back on a comfy seat.

RUTH THE TRUTH'S PSYCHIC DEVELOPMENT PLAN

Before you start this voyage of discovery I want you have a few things nearby – a pen, some paper, a tape recorder if possible and a glass of clear still water. You'll find out why later on.

1. A safe place: It is so important that you carry out this training in a warm and safe environment. It should be hot enough so that when you begin to train your psychic abilities and you lose body heat, which does happen, you stay warm and comfortable. By 'safe environment' I refer to the fact that you will be opening yourself to unknown elements and this may mean that you feel tired during a session. So you should be sitting comfortably in a chair which will allow you to fall asleep if the notion takes hold of you. Also, if you are feeling safe and secure, you will be able to work much more efficiently. There will be no holding back on your part.

I usually do all my psychic work in my office, which is in my bedroom. I sit in a comfortable chair which allows me to relax and work when the need arises. Your special place should also be full of things you can relate to and feel comfortable with. It may be a bedroom or study which has your stamp on it. Decide on the right place for you and remember that it should be clear of clutter so that that doesn't get in the way of your psychic flow. Also, psychic development can come with habit and doing your work in the same place each time will help this process. As soon as I enter my room for work I can feel my senses booting up for action.

I always light a candle before I start any psychic work. This is normally a lavender one, which helps me to focus my mind and puts me in the right mood.

2. *Relaxing:* Now it is true that many of us will have psychic pops or visions at times of intense stress, but to develop this skill to your best advantage you really need to relax your mind and body at the very start. I know from my own experience that once I have relaxed I feel my body becoming one big psychic radar and if you learn to do this you will find this happens too.

To begin with I always sit comfortably in my chair with my hands in my lap. I close my eyes and take one breath in and one breath out. I do this slowly several times until I feel my heart slowing down and my mind relaxing. I just sit still, listening to my breathing and imagining that with each breath in my psychic ability is being awakened ready for the job in hand. I also say a little prayer to my Maker to say thank you for giving me such a great gift and allowing me to help the people I am about to see or whose letters I am about to read. You can make your own one up but mine is the following:

'Thank you, God, for giving me this great gift of prophecy. Please help me to assist the people I am working with today.'

After this I am prepared to go on to the next stage, as you will be too.

3. *Clearing and stilling the mind:* This was always one of the most difficult parts of my psychic development. My mind has always been active and being a little hyperactive as a child I found it hard to be still. But nonetheless I have developed this so that my psychic abilities are at their best at each sitting.

I am always sitting at this point and have my eyes closed. Go ahead and do the same. What I do next is to imagine that all my problems, worries and fears are on sheets of paper. I then place each sheet in one of the drawers of a large chest of drawers. All my problems are now put away, to be dealt with later on if the need arises.

Then I imagine I am looking into the centre of an amethyst geode. This is a formation of amethyst which is cut in half to reveal hundreds of tiny crystals and looks like a beautiful cave. I imagine I am small enough to fit inside the cave and I am surrounded by the most beautiful purple crystals. You can use this imagery or there may be a safe place you can visit, perhaps a place from your childhood or a holiday destination you long to experience. As soon as I feel myself projected away to my safe cave I know that I am still, free of all my worries, and that my mind is clear and ready to accept psychic information.

4. *Psychic protection:* This is the most important stage in the process. I can't stress enough how vital it is to protect yourself when carrying out any of my exercises. You are training your senses to accept information from unknown sources most of the time and if you are not protected you can be harmed. I don't suggest that you can be harmed in a physical sense, but in an emotional and spiritual sense this can happen.

I remember that when I was a teenager I was asked by a guy at a party to do a reading for him. I felt sorry for him and could sense that his situation was desperate, so I began to read for him without my protective armour in place. After the session I felt very ill. Six weeks previously he had been at the home of an old schoolfriend and he had played the ouija board. Unfortunately he had had an entity latch on to his spiritual body and it was causing him great distress. Of course the entity then decided to attach itself to me, as I had no way of fighting it off without my usual safety cover. I felt ill for days and had the worst nightmares. Thankfully my gran was able to release me from its grip using some of her very own special magic. After that, I vowed never to do a reading or anything psychic without protection again.

If you have read books on psychic protection then you probably have a good understanding of what I am going to ask you to do at this stage of the process, although as usual you will find I do things in my own sweet way.

Sitting comfortably with your body relaxed, eyes closed and mind still, I want you to imagine that you have a torch just above the top of your head. It is pointing downwards and is switched off just now. Imagine that you have pressed the switch to turn it on and that a beam of light is shining down on you. Allow this bright white light to cover your whole body so that no part is hidden from it. You are covered in brilliant white light which is offering you spiritual, emotional and physical protection from all beings and elements. You can now open up your eyes ready for the next stage.

5. *Opening up your psychic senses*: You are sitting comfortably, you are relaxed and have a still quiet mind. Above all, you have your protective suit on. You are now ready to open up your psychic senses. For this you need to be able to open up one of your chakras.

The Chakra System

The chakra system originates from ancient India. The word 'chakra' means 'wheel' and it is believed that chakras are spinning vortices or swirls of energy in the body. Each chakra has a specific focus and they are all linked to physical functions as well as mental and emotional states. There are seven in all and they are located at different points along the spine.

The Chakra System

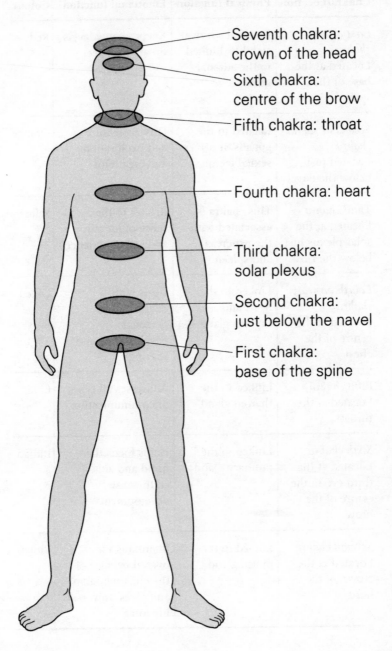

Seventh chakra:
crown of the head

Sixth chakra:
centre of the brow

Fifth chakra: throat

Fourth chakra: heart

Third chakra:
solar plexus

Second chakra:
just below the navel

First chakra:
base of the spine

Chakra/Location	Physical function	Emotional function	Colour
First or root chakra Located at the base of the spine	Physical survival, stability. Linked to the adrenal glands	Keeps energy levels on an even keel	Red
Second or sacral chakra Located just below the navel	Related to the gonads, it drives sexual feelings	Drives pleasure and exploration and creativity	Orange
Third chakra Located at the solar plexus just below the ribs	This chakra is associated with the pancreas and spleen	Relates to the sense of identity and self-confidence	Yellow
Fourth or heart chakra Located at the centre of the chest	Linked to the heart and thymus gland	Deals with relationships, personal development and sharing	Green
Fifth chakra Located at the throat	Linked to the thyroid gland	Addresses all types of communication	Blue
Sixth chakra Located at the third eye in the centre of the brow	Linked to the pituitary gland	Helps focus the mind and aids sixth-sense development	Indigo
Seventh chakra Located at the crown of the head	Linked to the pineal gland	Maintains the overall balance of the chakra system and gives universal life force	Violet

For you to unleash and enhance your psychic perception you need to be able to open up your sixth chakra. You can do this by imagining that on your forehead there is a doorway you can open up. This will activate your senses and allow you to take in information. Then open up your fourth chakra, which is located in the centre of your chest. This will advance your personal development and allow your experience to be harmonised in a loving, giving way. These are the two chakras I concentrate on when doing my work, as this allows me to work easily and methodically. I have found that opening all the chakras causes me to feel overloaded.

Once you have opened these chakras, you are ready to take in information.

6. 'Is there anybody there?': This is where you will need your pen and paper. I want you to jot down all the images that are coming into your head just now. They may be of family or friends doing something. What are they doing? Note it all down. What are you hearing? Are there any voices? What are they saying? Do you recognise them?

Take about 10 minutes and note down all that you see, hear, feel or smell. These are your 10 minutes of psychic discovery, so use them well. You never know, what you have sensed may be just the information you have been looking for. In some cases you may even feel that there is someone else in the room with you. Say hi, as this could well be your psychic guide who has come to help you out for the first time. Take note of what they look like or sound like. Better still, do they have a name and if so, do you know them? As you try to develop your senses further you may get help from them, perhaps each time or maybe only when you need them.

7. *Shut down:* Now you can take a sip of that pure still water I told you to have prepared. You have done a lot of work today and should be proud of yourself. But just as booting up your psychic system properly is important, so is shutting it down.

To do this you can use a trick I learned a while back. Sitting comfortably in your seat, give thanks for the information that you have received today. I always say something like: '*Thank you for giving me insight and guidance today.*' Then close your eyes and imagine that the torch on top of your head beaming its bright white light is switched off. This will allow you to come back to planet Earth ready to get on with the rest of your day.

You may feel a little tired just now, but as you practise more, your body will become more used to the whole process.

What special tools should you use?

I was born with psychic skills already tuned in, so to speak. That is why up until my friend brought me those witchdoctor bones I really hadn't thought about using anything to help it along – that is, except reading the tea leaves, which my gran taught me. But once you have practised my seven-point plan, you will come to what I call the 'How can I keep my interest in this alive?' stage. After many sessions with your pen and paper you will feel that the inspiration is perhaps dwindling, so it is a good idea to take up a way of fortune-telling to help you to develop your skills.

I have chosen the tea leaves as a good start as my family spent many nights huddled round my gran's fire listening to her teach us how to read the tea leaves. You may not even like tea, but read on anyway, as this is a fascinating way of reading someone else's future. Just bear in mind that the leaves must be read for the person who has drunk the cup of tea.

HOW TO READ THE TEA LEAVES

Reading the tea leaves has been a way of fortune-telling ever since man first discovered tea many moons ago. It was widely practised by Romanies and still is for both personal or client use. I think that the first time my gran showed me how to read the tea leaves I was around seven years of age. The whole ritual fascinated me and I am sure that if you like a cup of tea this may be the ideal way of developing your skills.

How to make the tea

Now you may wonder why I am explaining how to make

the tea, but the reason is simple: to get a proper reading you have to follow the ritual. Plus, how many of you out there use tea bags? If you do this when preparing the tea for a reading, then you are not going to get much information.

1. Fill your kettle with fresh water from the tap and pop it on to boil.

2. Get your cup, saucer, teapot, loose tea and milk ready. (A cup is better than a mug.)

3. Once the water comes to the boil, pour some into the teapot, swirl it around and then pour it out. This warms the pot ready for the tea – essential for a good cuppa!

4. Get your tea and put one teaspoonful in the pot for each person having a cup. Any type of tea can be used, but I find that the leaves of Darjeeling are the best for divination purposes.

5. Pour the water into the pot as soon as it comes to the boil. Then put the lid on the teapot and let the tea brew for a couple of minutes.

6. Pour your freshly brewed tea into the cups and add milk and sugar if required. Remember not to use a tea strainer!

Preparation of the tea for reading

As I have said before, when reading the tea leaves it is better to use a cup rather than a mug. This is because a mug's sides are too steep to get a good dispersal of leaves. Also, if the inside of the cup is plain, it will be easier to discern any shapes.

Once the person who is getting the reading has drunk their tea, ask them to swirl the remaining dregs of tea around three times *anti-clockwise* using their left hand (whether they are right or left-handed). Then ask them to turn the cup upside-down and again turn it three times *anti-clockwise* with their left hand. Once they have done this, turn the cup over and take a look inside.

The cup becomes the template for future events and shows when these events will take place. The handle signifies the enquirer and so leaves in or around this area concern them. The direct opposite side of the cup represents events affecting strangers. When you see pictures or symbols which point towards the enquirer, situations are entering their lives, and when they are pointing away, they are leaving them. The general consensus is that the bottom of the cup indicates sorrow and the rim joy.

The timing of events can be read in two different ways. You can either look at the circumference of the cup – tea leaves close to the handle indicate the near future and those further away show events in the distant future. Or, if you look at leaves in the whole cup, those in the bottom of the cup refer to the distant future, in the

Tea Cup Readings: See where the dregs of your tea leaves fall and match them to the areas shown in the cup representations below.

Where will the events take place?

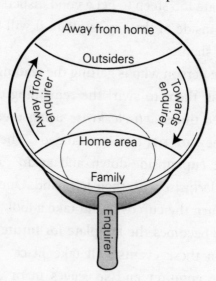

When will the events take place?

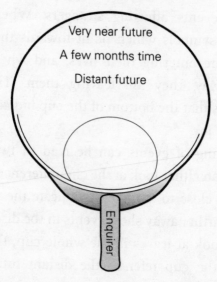

middle to events occurring in a few months and at the top to things happening in the near future.

Now all you have to do is study the cup very carefully from all angles. You will see images, symbols and pictures. I always have a pad and pencil at the ready to take down any notes. Jot down anything you see, as it will all have some meaning. I have compiled a list of popular symbols, but as you train your eye and psychic abilities you will be able to read what the tea leaves are telling you in a creative way. Keep an open mind and inspiration will guide you.

Tea leaf symbols and what they mean

Generally speaking, letters of the alphabet reveal the names of people important in the reading. Stalks always show people. The long ones usually indicate a man and the short ones a woman. My gran would always tell me that lucky signs were circles, rings, animals, crowns and flowers. To see the number 7 would be extremely lucky indeed. Triangles with the point upwards are also considered lucky omens. In fact a triangle can mean a win of some description. Squares mean protection or a change in circumstances. Little dots show money and if they appear on top of the tea before it is drunk it is a very good financial sign. More specific symbols are as follows:

Acorn: Business and financial success.
Aeroplane: A journey will be taken in the air. If broken, then be careful of silly accidents.

Angel: Good news is on the way. Your guardian angel is helping you out.

Arrow: Unpleasant news. Be prepared and it won't be so bad.

Axe: Difficulties will be overcome, but it will take a fight to reach a positive conclusion.

Bag: A trap is being set for you to fall into. Keep your eyes open and this will be dealt with.

Balloon: Freedom from all your current worries. You will succeed in business, but make sure your ideas are not stolen.

Bell: Unexpected good news. A celebration which will allow you to see many old friends and family.

Bird: Someone is bringing you good news and you will be able to act on it.

Boat: A visit from a friend. Travel across the sea to another country is likely.

Book: Wisdom or an older person giving you advice.

Car: Good fortune for things moving forward. Mechanical problems.

Cat: Treachery – watch out for false friends who are up to no good.

Circle: Success, the completion of a project or news of a baby.

Dagger: Danger ahead, so beware of reckless behaviour.

Dog: A good and faithful friend who may need your help to overcome a problem.

Egg: Fertility and news of a pregnancy. Business plans being accepted.

Fire: Don't be too hasty. Think before you leap into action.

Fish: Good fortune for all around you. A new job is likely to come your way.

Flower: Your wishes coming true. A child who has more wisdom than their years allow.

Fruit: Prosperity which will allow you to put plans into action at long last.

Gate: A new phase of life. The transition is likely to bring rewards.

Grapes: A love affair is developing which will bring happiness.

Hand: If open, a friendship; if closed, an argument will ensue.

Heart: Pleasure, love and friendship will be found.

Hill: Obstacles and setbacks are likely, so be prepared for the worst.

House: Security will be found, so learn to relax in time. Moving house is likely.

Ladder: Promotion will bring with it deserved success.

Letter: Important news is likely by letter.

Moon: Romance with a rich individual will bring happiness.

Palm tree: Honour for your charitable work and concerns.

Ring: At the top of the cup, a marriage; at the bottom, an engagement. If broken, a broken relationship.

Scales: Legal matters will be dealt with. If balanced, justice will prevail; if not, it won't.

Snake: An enemy is nearby, so be extra vigilant.

Spade: Hard work will bring success in time.

Star: Hope and health will make life much better very soon.

Train: Time to move forward in life. Stop thinking of past events.

Tree: Changes for the better. Home improvements will be considered.

Umbrella: If open, irritation is likely, so be prepared; if closed, things will settle in a short time.

Volcano: Emotionally, a very tense time. Eruptions are likely.

Waterfall: Luck in competitions and in all walks of life.

Wheel: If complete, good fortune will be on its way; if broken, disappointment.

Wings: Messages are likely from many sources. The news may be good or bad depending on where the wings are in the cup.

Witch: A nasty woman will cause problems if she is allowed to do so.

This is only a selection of symbols but will give you a good start in reading the tea leaves. For further information, consult the 'where to buy' section and the list of books at the back of the book.

This chapter has introduced you to the possibility that you can develop your own psychic abilities. It will open up a whole new intriguing world to you, a world in which many things are possible.

CHAPTER 5

Love:
How to Find It
and Keep It

I MET MY HUSBAND when I was 16 years of age. Two years before I had ever set eyes on him my gran read my tea leaves. She saw 'a boy with curly hair and a shy personality', which interested me, as I did have a soft spot for curls. Two years later my boyfriend and I arranged a blind date for my friend and his friend. They were to meet on a busy Saturday afternoon and I went into Glasgow with my pal for support. After leaving her alone to wait for this new guy, I saw a boy walking towards me. I stared at him, as at 16 I was a bit pushy. He stared back and I thought, 'Wow, he is gorgeous.' Some time later I met my friend and her new man, as we had agreed earlier, and I couldn't believe it when it was the same guy I had eyed up earlier. Luckily my friend didn't like Ronald and after she chucked him, he phoned me and asked me out. I waited two weeks and let him sweat, then phoned back and accepted his offer. Thirteen years and two children later, the rest, as they say, is history. And if you are asking, was my gran right? Yes, Ronald had curly hair and was very shy.

We don't all have grans who can look into a cup of tea leaves to reassure us that we will find love, but you can learn subtle ways of attracting that special someone and then developing the relationship until marriage is a real option, if this is what you want.

Old wives' tales

Many of the old wives' tales from the past are related to the subject of love. My gran was always full of these as they had been relayed to her by her grannie and so forth. One thing she told me was that the best aphrodisiac is not oysters or strawberries, but a plant called lovage. This is found mainly on shorelines or sea cliffs. My gran would tell me that this was used in a hot broth to give a sense of well-being and if served to the correct person, love could be in the air. Orchids in a room would also elicit a sense of sensuality just by their very shape and aroma. If you wanted to know who your partner would be, you could cut the herb yarrow from the garden before sunrise and then place it under your pillow. That night you would dream of your future lover.

Food seemed to be used in many different ways in the old rituals of finding that special someone. Apples were a popular divining tool, especially in Scotland. My gran often told me that if you took an apple and carefully peeled it so that the skin was intact, then threw it over your left shoulder, it would reveal the initial of your true soulmate. Whenever I tried this the initial was always difficult to decipher, so you had to use your imagination!

All of these ways of finding love were often used in the olden days because there was less travel and movement of people then, so the chances of finding someone were more restricted. These old ways may sound a bit strange to us now, but they were thought to be helpful at the time.

Helping love to enter your life

So, OK, perhaps the old ways of discovering who your lover will be aren't very practical in this day and age, but there are still love potions and charms that you can use to help you out. Nowadays with the Internet and telecommunications as they are, relationships are becoming depersonalised. For this chapter I would ask you to get back to basics, that is, use your instincts and senses to guide you on your path. The love potion I am about to divulge is a family recipe which has worked on many levels for friends and family. You can use it or modify it to suit your needs, but it is potent, so be warned!

RUTH THE TRUTH'S LOVE POTION

This one was passed down by my Turkish grannie, who seemingly kept a note of it all her days written in cross-stitch on a silk handkerchief.

Take a bottle either of sweet dessert wine such as Muscat or of non-alcoholic grape juice. Add to it a couple of sprigs of fresh rosemary, from the garden if you have it or if not the supermarket variety will do. Then add some red rose petals and finally a teaspoonful of cinnamon. Place the bottle in the fridge and let it sit for two hours. Then take it out and have a drink of it whenever you are going on a night out. Remember to strain the wine before you drink it. I use a tea strainer.

People who have tried this have felt that their charms have increased on their night out and often they have met someone as a consequence. If you want, you can share the potion with single friends who want to benefit from its power.

Love potions are fun to devise. You don't have to stick to this one, as you may have a better idea of what would make you tick.

Now from love potions to love charms. Love charms have been around since time began and in general they are something personal which allows you to focus on the subject of love. My gran once told me that when she was a child of 10 an old aunt of hers picked up a large pebble whilst they were out on a walk in the woods one windy autumn Saturday, saying that once they got home they would make a wishing stone. As promised, once they got home they both sat in front of the hot coal fire and held the pebble in turn. They thought of various shapes and then painted these on to the pebble in bright colours.

Once they had finished the old aunt held the stone and said: '*Wishing stone, wishing stone, make my wish come true. Wishing stone, wishing stone, make my love be you.*' She then told my gran that the stone would make her wishes come true and if she ever wanted to find her true love she only had to hold it and ask it the way she had been shown. My gran kept the stone until she was an old lady.

HOW TO MAKE YOUR OWN WISHING PEBBLE LOVE CHARM

You will need:
★ a stone pebble the size of your palm, collected on a walk on a windy day, preferably in autumn or around dusk
★ a blue pen
★ paper
★ a paintbrush
★ enamel paints

Method

To find your stone pebble you need to set aside time for a walk. During the walk think about what you want to do, so that you will find a pebble special to you.

When you get home, choose a time when you will have peace and quiet to do the process properly.

Now, when you are ready, sit comfortably with your eyes closed, and think about who you want the wishing pebble to bring. It may be a stranger or you may already know the person. Imagine colours, patterns and shapes representing your special person. Once you have done this, open your eyes and take your pen and paper and draw what you imagined. This will be your own unique imprint that will relate to your wish.

Now transfer your design on to the pebble using the enamel paints. Make sure the whole pebble is covered, so you will have to wait till the top half dries then do the bottom half.

When this is all done, make up your own incantation to summon up the spirit of love to activate your charm. Then, preferably on a new moon at 7 p.m., the loving hour, hold the stone and recite your incantation. The magical pebble will now be able to make your wishes come true.

SOWING THE SEEDS OF LOVE

I have already mentioned how important food is in the rituals of love. Another very old way of attracting a lover is by using the power of your green fingers, namely growing the aphrodisiac herb basil from seed. This little gem of a method has its roots in an old Italian custom, but has also been used extensively across the Mediterranean. I am sure that my Turkish grannie would have known about this one as well.

You will need:
★ a small terracotta pot
★ some earth from your garden or a friend's
★ some basil seeds
★ 2 red candles
★ 2 silver-coloured candlesticks

Method

On a full moon, take a few basil seeds and plant them in your terracotta pot with your special soil. Once you have done this, light your two candles and then ask that the seeds of love grow and grow. Every second day, water the seeds and as you do so say: *'Bring me a lover sweet and kind, bring me a lover not just in my mind.'*

By the time the seeds have grown, which normally takes around three to five months, it is said that you will have captured your lover's heart. You now make a meal with the basil and share it with them. This is a very romantic charm and although it does take a bit of time, I have it on good authority that it works.

Letting love blossom

By now, if you have been following my pearls of wisdom, I would expect you to have the man or woman of your dreams. It will have been hard work, but well worth it. The next stage I want to develop with you is the courting. Now you may think that a word such as 'courting' doesn't have a place in 21st-century society, but I would disagree. In our modern world things are too rushed and the emphasis seems to be on how quickly it can all be done. I want to slow things down so that love grows slowly but surely.

If the person you have met and liked is right for you, your gut instinct should tell you so. Now you need to harness the power of love and you can do this using old customs and rituals passed down to me by both my Scottish and Turkish grandmothers. The first one comes from Turkey and originated in the harems of Saudi Arabia. It is the Turkish love massage. Secondly, I will explain how to set up your very own love altar where you can pray and ask for things in regard to your relationship. And finally in this section we will turn to my favourite subject – food – with a feast to tickle the tastebuds and other extremities!

TURKISH LOVE MASSAGE

This will blow your lover's mind, as it will help them to relax and become aware of all the positive aspects of your relationship. It is also great if you have been feeling low or if your lover's libido has not been on form. It will allow you to heighten the senses ready for a night of sheer delight. A friend of my Turkish grannie gave this recipe to me, although neither of them ever admitted to using it.

You will need:
★ a small plate or saucer
★ a small plastic funnel
★ a 25 ml (1 fl oz) brown glass bottle (available from chemists)
★ rose oil (not cheap but very effective)
★ jasmine oil (again not cheap but necessary)
★ 4 needles of rosemary (garden fresh or bought fresh)
★ grapeseed oil

Method

Take your glass bottle and add 20 ml (just less than 1 fl oz) of grapeseed oil to it, using the small plastic funnel. Then add 4 drops of rose oil, 4 drops of jasmine oil and finally the rosemary and leave it to infuse for 3 hours at room temperature.

Once you are ready, get your partner to lie comfortably either on the bed or on the floor. Make sure that you are comfortable yourself and that you don't strain your back. It is also important that the room you are in is warm, as you don't want goosebumps getting in the way of your fun!

Take the bottle of oil, turn it round three times

clockwise on the palm of your hand and say: '*Oil of love, make this time a delight. Oil of love, make me his/her Turkish delight.*' Then pour some oil on to a saucer and take some between your palms and fingers.

It is now time for you to start the massage. I would suggest you start at the back and work your way round, letting your imagination run wild. The results, I am sure, will be electrifying, so be prepared for a long sleepless night – for all the best reasons, of course!

MAKING A LOVE ALTAR

I am a great believer in the power of an altar. I have had one since I can remember, as my gran always used to say how important it was as a focus in a room. An altar is a platform to carry out rituals. It is a place you can turn to when you want to concentrate on certain aspects of your life. I have two altars in my home. One is a religious one, where I pray, and the other is for my wishing work. In this case you want a platform which will signify your relationship and the love that comes from it.

You will need:
★ objects which symbolise your love and relationship,
such as photos, mementoes, etc
★ 2 red candles anointed with rose oil
★ 2 silver-coloured candlesticks
★ a short piece of red ribbon with a knot in it

Method

Look at your whole living space and decide where you want your altar to be. It could be at a window in your room or on a coffee table in the lounge. Anywhere is fine as long as you know it will be safe, secure and above all a zone of still calm when required.

Anoint your candles with rose oil, which basically means massaging a couple of drops of oil on to them. Place them in the candlesticks and put them in your altar space. Place your mementoes between the candles and finally place the red ribbon with a knot in it beside these.

You now have an altar and to activate it you need to sit at it on the night of a new moon at 10 p.m. This is the best possible time to sanctify your space and allow it to be used for the purpose of relationship growth and renewal. Whenever you feel the relationship isn't going the way you have planned or when you have had a quarrel, you should light your candles, sit at the altar and ask that you be assisted in riding the storm.

The altar is your own intimate place and it is up to you to develop a ritual which works for you. You can think of it as a blank canvas. It is a simple and beautiful way of being able to sit and reflect on your relationship.

PUTTING THE SPICE INTO YOUR RELATIONSHIP RECIPE

Food is at the heart of the art of seduction. Throughout history it has been used to symbolise all manner of things to do with the quest to find a soulmate. So many cultures reveal its importance through their ceremonies such as wedding banquets. When you first meet the person of your dreams I wager that one of the first things you do is to go out for a meal together. You will have heard the way to a man's heart is through his stomach. I hope that I can show you that this is true with my next ritual. The recipe was used by my Turkish forefathers to keep their love lives on the boil. Prepare the following dish the day before you wish to eat it.

You will need:

★ 4 tsp of sunflower oil

★ 3 whole cloves

★ a small piece of cinnamon bark

★ 1 green cardamom pod

★ 3 large white onions

★ 1 tsp each of ground cumin, coriander, ginger, turmeric and salt

★ ¼–1 tsp of chilli powder, to taste

★ 0.5 kg (1 lb) of meat, fish or vegetables

★ 3 peeled whole cloves of garlic

★ a large non-stick pot

Method

Put the oil into the pot and heat it, then add the cloves, cinnamon and cardamom. After 3 minutes add the chopped onions and cook on a medium heat for around 5 minutes. Mix in all the other spices. Cook on a low heat for 10 minutes, stirring occasionally. Add the meat, fish or vegetables and finally the garlic. Stir well and add enough water to cover. Simmer for 30 minutes for vegetables and 1½ hours for meat and fish.

Once the food is simmering, make up your own mantra to seal it with love. I would normally use: '*Spice and food, make my lover good.*' Just use your own imagination at this stage.

Once the food is cooked, let it cool then transfer it to the fridge until required.

On the night of your spicy meal for two use oils in a burner to set the mood. Patchouli, cinnamon or musk are ideal, but have fun finding a blend that suits you both. Light red candles around the room and have calming music drift over you while you eat. Serve the meal with basmati rice and remember to have wine for toasting the relationship. I am sure that following this old feast you'll find that food won't be the only thing on your mind all night.

What can you do if it all goes pear-shaped?

While courting, you will be learning a lot about each other. This will mean that the inevitable will happen – you will have arguments from time to time. If you do have a wee tiff, there are certain things you can do to soften the blow and patch things up.

Whenever Ronald and I had an argument when we were dating it would normally be my fault. This was due to the fact I had a strong forthright personality and to a certain extent I still do. I remember once being very upset as Ronald and I had fallen out. My gran told me to take two slices of wholemeal bread and a white ribbon. Once I had collected these I was to find my favourite photo of Ron and I as a couple. The photo was to be placed between the slices of bread and tied together with the white ribbon. I looked at her in disbelief but did as she said, as she had never let me down before. Then I placed my unusual sandwich on my love altar. Within 12 hours Ronald had shown up with a bunch of flowers in one hand and a new CD in the other.

You may laugh at my gran's unusual demands, but her method does work to this day.

If you fall out with your loved one over something silly, just write down what the argument was about on a piece of plain white paper with a red pen. Then, when your lover isn't looking, put it securely under their pillow. Before you go to bed at night, go to your altar and ask your guides to help build a bridge to reseal your love. In the morning I am sure the argument will have been forgotten.

Big shiny rings and things

Betrothal, engagement call it what you will, the next stage from courting if things go to plan is the big 'C' – commitment.

Finding your soulmate will not have been easy and I am sure that there will have been many trials and tribulations on the way. I was out on my first date with Ronald and within two hours I knew that we would marry. When I told him this I guess he must have thought that I was mad, but six weeks later we were engaged. Ronald had to ask my dad for my hand in marriage. In fact he took my dad out for a quiet Sunday afternoon drink and game of snooker – very west of Scotland. To take your future father-in-law for a drink to ask for his daughter's hand in marriage is in fact an old custom that has its roots in the Highlands. Normally the couple's friends would assemble at the girl's home. One spokesman from her beau's side would come forward and ask the father if he needed help on the farm or factory, etc. If the wedding was agreed, the father would set the date then and there. Nowadays this tradition seems to be diminishing – that is, unless your dad is Turkish, like mine. He likes tradition and why not?

The engagement ring is an integral part of this process. It signifies a union of two souls. When I got engaged all my friends and family would ask to try my ring on. When they did, they would turn it round on their finger three times clockwise and make a wish for luck. This is a custom which has its roots in the Roman Empire, with their love of jewels and belief in the symbolism of rings.

Once you have the ring on your finger it is a very exciting time, as from that date it is usually all hands on deck preparing for the wedding. This was certainly the case for me and as I was only 17 at the time of my engagement, I needed a lot of help. One of the first things my gran did, apart from congratulate me, was to tell me about the bottom drawer. It was an old Celtic custom for the bride to have a wedding kist, or chest, containing table linen and bedding for her home. It is now called a bottom drawer. My bottom drawer was full to the brim within a day of my getting engaged, so it ended up as two double drawers! As customs go, this is a good practical one.

Getting engaged is a very exciting time in a relationship. By this time you realise that you want to spend the rest of your life with that special person.

Pre-wedding celebrations

Now I am assuming that if you are getting engaged you will be getting married. I say this as I have known people to become engaged with no intention of ever getting married. If you are on track and are getting married, though, then this next section is for you.

As with the wedding itself, the pre-wedding time has many traditions and ceremonies associated with it. For a start you will have the hen night and stag night, which are still a part of British culture, then the show of presents, or 'wedding shower', as it is called in the States. Finally, if you are a Turkish bride, you are expected to cry the night before your wedding. All will be revealed . . .

HEN NIGHTS AND STAG NIGHTS

I had a fairly traditional hen night. I was dressed head to toe in suspenders, ripped stockings, bin bags, balloons and of course who could forget the customary 'L' plate and veil? Make-up was loud and bright. I looked like the bride of Frankenstein's monster. I was walked out of my home and paraded to all the neighbours by my sisters and family. At the first house I came to I knocked on the door and asked for a jam sandwich, or 'jeely piece', as it is traditionally called. I carried a baby's potty full of salt. This was to collect money from the men I stopped and kissed on my way into town. The pot of salt signifies the bride-to-be's fertility and future wealth. The procession into town is not done quietly, but to the accompaniment of pots and pans being banged with spoons.

Once we got to town, which was a two-mile walk, it was time to hit the pubs, where the kissing for money continued. All in the best possible taste of course. I didn't do too badly either, as at the end of the night my potty held £140, which went towards my honeymoon. Nowadays, though, most brides will not opt for the ridicule of the traditional hen night but will be seen sipping Chardonnay in a wine bar with some chums.

As with the hen night, the stag night is still found in most parts to this day. This is the night when the poor old groom is expected to suffer at the hands of his so-called friends. Many years ago it was traditionally held the night before the wedding, but after stories of grooms being lost or too ill to attend the wedding, it is now thought better to do it a couple of weeks before. Victims of the most extreme pranks have found themselves naked and penniless in train stations miles from home. My friend's husband was even tarred and feathered. He came from Aberdeen and that is a normal occurrence in the north-east of Scotland. My own poor husband had a stag night, and to this day if you mention Newcastle brown ale he feels sick.

These pre-wedding celebrations stem from traditional gatherings which were meant to give the bride or groom once last chance to see what life would be like if they didn't get hitched.

PRE-WEDDING TEARS FROM TURKEY

On some of my visits to Turkey I have witnessed the most wonderful parties, called 'henna parties'. This is when all the local girls, mothers, aunties and so on meet up and celebrate a forthcoming wedding with food and tea. All the girls, including the bride, must have their hands and feet painted with henna. This dates back to the early 17th century, when henna was considered to give women healing qualities, including fertility and good health. The henna party involves lots of singing and dancing, without alcohol because of the Islamic culture, and at the end of the night the bride-to-be is made to cry. This isn't a bad thing, but is seen as a very good omen of how the marriage will be. The more tears the better. The idea is that the bride is crying because she will be leaving her mother to start a new life with her husband's family.

THE SHOW OF PRESENTS

The show of presents is the chance for the bride to invite all her female friends and family members to see her wedding gifts. It is less popular than it used to be in Britain, but in America it is still a part of pre-wedding culture and is called a wedding shower. It also allows the bride to see all her female nearest and dearest before her big day. At this point she usually needs their support.

ALL IN WHITE WITH MR OR MRS RIGHT

The wedding can be seen as the prize at the end of all the hard work you have been through in finding and keeping your partner. I was engaged at 17 and married at 19, on 6th August 1988. Thirteen years later I am still happily married, while many people I know who married after me are no longer together.

I remember my wedding as if it were yesterday. I was married in my local church and had a reception in a posh hotel in Glasgow. I wore something old, something new, something borrowed and something blue. I also had a piece of silver in my shoe, which in my case was 5 pence. My grannie would have gone spare if I hadn't been superstitiously correct. My something old was my grannie's silk handkerchief; something new was my dress; something borrowed was my mum's pendant and something blue was a garter. Also, my wedding car was decked in white ribbons, which is said to bring luck on your wedding day. The ceremony was traditional and the meal was too. Where my wedding would differ from perhaps your own was that at the reception I was given gold jewellery and had money pinned on to my dress at the first dance. These are all old Turkish customs, which are great from the bride's point of view. My dress was brilliant white, a tradition that only came into fashion when Queen Victoria decided it was the colour she wanted to wear for her own wedding.

Once married, my gran told me to protect what I had and so she passed on her very last pearl of wisdom before she sadly died a few years later. 'The day you get back from honeymoon,' she told me, 'make a friendship bracelet long enough so that when you halve it, it will be enough for two.' That is what I did and Ronald and I wore the bracelets until they wore away. I often think that this strong and powerful amulet has helped strengthen my marriage.

If you would like to make bracelets of your own, this is how to do it:

A LOVE CHARM TO PROTECT
A RELATIONSHIP

You will need:
★ a leather thong or fine ribbon
★ beads, shells or charms

Method

Spend some time thinking about what you want the bracelets to do. Then choose what you want to have on them.

Cut a piece of the leather thong or ribbon so that there is enough to make two bracelets. Tie a knot at the end of the thong, then add the beads, or whatever you like: it is totally up to you. Tie knots all the way along to secure the beads.

Once you have about 2.5–5 cm (1–2 in) left, tie an end knot and then tie both ends together. Sit with the charm in your palm and utter under your breath, '*Charm, strengthen my union so no one can break it.*' Then present it to your partner. Cut the band in half and tie the ends together to make two bracelets. Keep them on until they naturally break or fall apart.

You can do this again whenever you feel you need the protection.

Finally ...

This is a powerful chapter. It takes you from a person in search of a soulmate to the final union of two souls through marriage. You can use any section as and when you need it or skip ones you feel you don't require. Remember, love is great and all of us deserve to be loved, so go out and get it.

CHAPTER 6

A Happy Family and a Happy Home

MY WHOLE LIFE revolves around my family. My children are the most important, as I would give up my life for them. In this chapter I want to take a look at how harmony in the home can be achieved using my old wise ways and rituals. From how to get pregnant to how to calm a relative, this chapter has it all. I will also look at how to make the home a positive place to live in, using techniques my gran taught me.

First things first, one of my favourite subjects – babies and how to have one. By now you should have a good idea of how to find and develop a special relationship. The next step, once you are in this stable union, is having a child. It is a natural instinct which comes to nearly everyone. When I first married I had no intention of having a baby, but within four years maternal feelings seemed to come out of nowhere.

I was blessed in that I fell pregnant very easily, but alas this is not the case for everyone. For many women who have written to me over the years there is nothing physically wrong. This is where more traditional methods come into their own, as they can give Mother Nature a helping hand. If there is a problem physically, then fertility clinics do have a place, but this isn't the case every time. I have some simple natural ways to help you get pregnant, including one to help with a man's role.

Fertility matters

I certainly took my fertility for granted, but some people need a wee bit of help. My simple rituals have worked for people I know, but there can be no guarantees. It is up to Mother Nature herself.

The first thing you must do if you are having fertility problems is to stay calm. Fretting about the situation won't change anything. Conception is a delicate process and you must get into the correct frame of mind. Being happy, positive and chilled can bring you results. Guided imagery will help you connect with Mother Nature. Here is a simple exercise for you to do.

GUIDED IMAGERY FOR A POSITIVE MIND

Step 1: Lie down on your bed and make yourself comfortable. Make sure that nothing distracts you for at least 10 minutes. Close your eyes and place your arms to your sides. Listen to your breathing and concentrate on each breath as it goes in and out.

Step 2: Slowly breathe in and out four times, then start to imagine that you are in beautiful woodland. The trees are towering above you, protecting you from the bright sunlight. Underfoot there are plants, grass and moss. As you walk you can hear the crunch of the fallen twigs and soil. You can smell the ferns, the woody fragrant trees and the soil. You can see small animals – a leaping green frog, a happy squirrel or a shy fox. You are one with nature and you are at peace.

Step 3: Take a walk through the wood and at the end you will come to a clearing where the sun's golden rays are peeking through the canopy of tall trees. On the other side is the most glorious landscape. There are green fields and cows and sheep grazing on the hills. The sun is shining and all is well.

Step 4: Now you walk back through the wood, slowly taking in all of nature's wonders. You come to the tree where you started and feel happy with your walk.

Step 5: Now slowly come to your senses. Stretch your whole body like a cat. Wriggle your hands, fingers and toes. Finally, slowly open your eyes. Become aware of your surroundings and just take a few minutes to get yourself together. Sit up and slowly get to your feet. A glass of chilled water will help to make you alert and ready to continue your day. But no rushing about, or you will undo your good work!

I suggest you do this exercise every day to get yourself ready for conception. Also, sex should not be staged or planned. It is a natural process for all to enjoy. Make it spontaneous and funny.

Now you are ready to boost your fertility. I have some real gems of wisdom to teach you, which I hope will help out in your quest for parenthood. All of my simple rituals should be performed on a waxing moon – that is, just before the full moon – to help their effectiveness.

BABIES' BOOTEES

My mum told me this very simple old wives' tale when a friend of mine was having difficulty getting pregnant. She explained to her that she needed to learn to knit. Once she had done this she was to knit a little pair of bootees, preferably in white wool. After this she was to place them under her pillow and *refrain* from sex for seven days. On the eighth day the ban was lifted and six weeks later she was pregnant. This is a simple old custom which might just help.

HONEY NUTS

And I don't mean cornflakes ... My dad relayed this one to me, which surprised me, as I didn't know he knew anything about the subject. He remembers having heard it when he was a boy. Its roots are definitely Turkish, as it contains the country's favourite delicacies – honey, yoghurt and hazelnuts. These foods represent fertility at its most basic level. Honey is considered to be an aphrodisiac and to have healing properties. The yoghurt should be ewe's milk and signifies the birth of lambs in springtime, which in turn symbolises new life and cycles. The nuts are a symbol of fertility and reflect the human reproductive organs. So all in all, this is one hell of a fertility boost. Both men and women can benefit from this.

You will need:
★ pasteurised ewe's milk yoghurt
★ crushed hazelnuts
★ clear honey

Method

Once you have made the decision that you want to become a parent, you need to include the above ingredients into your daily diet. In Turkey they would make a sweet by mixing some honey in a bowl with the yoghurt, then top it off by sprinkling the chopped hazelnuts on it. This tastes good, but is also nutritional and with any luck will help to get your bits and bobs in working order for making a baby.

FERTILITY ALTAR

You will realise by now how much I enjoy my altars. They are a focus for when you want to just sit and be still or to evoke help from a higher source.

A fertility altar is just a simple platform for you to worship your virility. In African culture, which is diverse, women who want to harness their fertility will often have an altar and worship their fertility goddess. I have my success and wishing altar on my windowsill, but your altar can be set up anywhere, as long as it is safe.

It is simple to create your own fertility altar. I will give you an idea of what you should use and you can add to it as you wish. Let your intuition guide you.

You will need:

★ 1 moonstone

★ 1 rose quartz crystal

★ 2 acorns

★ 2 pomegranates or 2 passionfruit

★ 1 goddess of fertility statue

★ 2 green candles

★ 2 silver-coloured candlesticks

The fruit used should have many seeds in it, so if pomegranate or passionfruit are not available, then choose something with seeds. Fertility figures can be purchased in many New Age stores, but I also give a list of suppliers at the back of the book.

Method

Set this up, as I said before, on a waxing moon. Make sure your chosen place is clean and dust free. Balance is all-important here. Place the moonstone and crystal at either side of your space. Then beside these put the acorns, fruit and then candles. In the middle will be your fertility goddess, as she is the focus of your altar.

Each day at 7.30 a.m. and 7.30 p.m. sit quietly at your altar and ask for help from the goddess. Then light your candles and state your intentions. This is a lovely way of focusing your mind in a positive way to help you conceive.

After carrying out my old methods I hope you will be successful in your quest for a child. But once you actually have children, what do you do with them? And how do you achieve a happy home? Using my mystical skills, I will show you how.

Happy families

With two sisters and a mum and dad, I have never found my family life boring. In fact we have the most amazing bust ups, but within a couple of minutes they are normally forgotten. I have always felt secure in my family unit and this has carried on in the way I raise my own children. Here I shall show you how to use simple rituals and old traditions to keep your family strong, safe and above all harmonious. Of course I also ask for God's help every night.

FAMILY PROTECTION

As parents it is our job to protect our family. Since the dawn of man protection has been a priority. Just because we live in a so-called civilised and technological society doesn't mean that this should have changed. Danger and negativity are still around us, only nowadays they come from people who want to cause us harm and from the environment we live in.

Protection has been all around me since I was a child. I remember my father pinning a blue glass bauble on my little cardigans and uttering Islamic mantras. Some years later I discovered that it was in fact an evil eye he was pinning on me. The evil eye is a Middle Eastern and Turkish superstition which dates back centuries. The eye represents the eye of God and pinning it on yourself signifies that God is watching out for you and making sure evil is not allowed to affect you.

I always have an evil eye in my car, house and purse. One of my friends swears by the one I got her on a trip to Turkey. One afternoon it fell off the dashboard of her car and on to the road. As she was driving at the time, she had no hope of retrieving it. Two days later a car went straight into the back of her. Shaken, the first thing she told me was to get her another evil eye. I duly did this, as I have a bag full of them in my house for emergencies. Thankfully she hasn't had any crashes since.

As well as my house having a stack of evil eyes for protection I also have a rowan tree. The rowan has been long believed to offer protection, as it is supposed to be favoured by angels and fairies. If they were attracted to a rowan near your home, it was said that they would offer your home protection.

The willow tree is also blessed with protective powers. Its potency was first recognised by the Picts, who used arrows of willow to kill enemies. The Celts also told of the willow's help in battles and in hunting animals. Its magical properties seem assured, if you believe the tales that go along with it. This is why at Christmas and Easter you see willow wreaths on doors. The custom stems from times when these trees where seen as highly spiritual commodities.

You can have added protection in your home by planting either a willow or rowan tree in your garden. If you don't have a garden or enough space, then a wreath on your door will do. To give it extra strength, tie golden ribbons around it.

Happy harmonious children

Now that you have a good idea of how to protect your home from a traditional angle, we can turn our attention to children. I love kids, especially my own, as they give me no end of joy. All you want for your children is happiness. My favourite sound in the whole wide world is that of children laughing. This is especially true of my own. From a young age allow your children to express themselves. Let them talk to you and share ideas.

THE HAPPY SUNSHINE CEREMONY

There is the most wonderful ceremony you can do during the summer months with your kids. My gran did it with me when I was eight years of age, just as she had been shown by her gran. All you need is a meadow or garden full of daisies and a wonderful imagination. This celebration of sunshine evokes feelings of happiness in anyone who carries it out. It also helps children to develop a sense of nature.

You will need:
★ a field, meadow or garden with fresh daisies
growing in it
★ a gold or yellow purse or pouch
★ a small citrine quartz crystal

Method

During the summer months, wait until you get a really bright sunny day. Knowing Britain, you may have to be patient for this, but if you live abroad it may not pose such a problem. Go out to your garden or enjoy a walk in a park, meadow or field. Anywhere there are daisies growing wild will do.

Play a game with your children of 'Let's find the daisies'. Once you have found your crop of daisies, sit down with your children and tell them the story of how special the daisy is. The story goes a little like this, but you can add or change parts of it as you wish:

'In days of old, knights would wear a daisy chain given to them by their fair maidens as a token of their love. If a knight wore a chain for his brave battles, then his heart was the lady's. The damsel would wear a garland of daisies he had made her. The daisy was said to possess magic, as it was protected by the fairies and the little folk. No matter how many times it was trampled underfoot by horses, cattle or people, it would resurrect itself the next spring as if by magic.'

Show the children how to make a daisy chain and then let them make their own. It is great to see them having such fun. Then place the garlands on their heads like crowns or around their necks like beautiful golden jewels. Allow them to make up their own stories using their vivid imaginations. Then stand in a circle holding hands. Look up to the sky and thank Mother Earth for her magnificent achievement in making such a strong but simple little flower.

When it is time to go home, take the chains and place them in the golden pouch for luck. Make sure the citrine quartz is in the pouch too, as this will keep the daisy chain energised with solar energy. This will now be a powerful amulet or charm to protect your children.

TAKING AWAY A CHILD'S TROUBLES

Sometimes children get sad and worry about things. I know my children do, and a silly thing to an adult can be a huge thing to a child. If you sense that your child is unhappy – and your intuition will be developing as you learn from this book – then follow this simple exercise. All you need for this is paper, some pens and a magic wand. I made my wand by taking a wooden spoon and painting it black with a white tip.

Explain to your child that they have to write down a wish list of things they would like to happen in their lives. What do they want to be better at school? Is there anyone in their lives causing them problems? Whatever it is, just get them to add them to their wish list. Then wave your magic wand and speak to them about the list. Explain to them that the problems can be resolved if the list is realistic. When I was a child I remember writing down that I was being bullied at school and I wanted it to stop. My gran made it clear to me that she would help me out, which she did. I couldn't have told anyone about it, but writing it down like this seemed easier.

Happy relations

I don't know of any family which doesn't have a few differences of opinion from time to time. Difficulties may arise unexpectedly and they have to be dealt with. Where my mum and gran were concerned, fights would never last for long. It wasn't until I was in my twenties that my gran told me her little secret – she had special rituals to get people back on speaking terms and to dampen down any explosive situations. Just her special words of wisdom would sort things out at times. I use her wisdom whenever I feel that family relations are becoming strained.

Whenever there are any family disagreements, do the following ritual on a waning moon. A waning moon is just after the full moon. It helps to direct things away from you. Throughout this book I mention the moon a lot, as she exerts a special power over us all. This ritual helps to make your home a positive place in which difficult relatives will find that their negative ideas about you just melt away.

RELATIVE MOON RITUAL

You will need:
★ fresh red and yellow flowers – whatever is
in season
★ patchouli incense
★ a gold or yellow candle
★ a dish of lavender water
★ a glass vase
★ a compass

Method

The ritual should be carried out on a waning moon so
that negative emotions are cast away. The flowers should
be placed at the most southerly part of the home. If in
doubt, you can use a compass just to make sure. Then
take the incense and put this at the most easterly part of
the home. The gold/yellow candle should be at the
window of the home which receives the most light and
finally the lavender water should be placed in the living-
room. This represents the soul of the family. Each object
you have placed represents an element and this gives a
note of balance to the ritual:

Flowers: Earth
Incense: Air
Golden candle: Fire
Lavender water: Water

Once all of this is in place, light the candle and the incense and sit quietly and think about the positive contribution you want to make to your relatives' lives. Sense the lunar energy activating each element represented by the objects. This will change negative emotions to positive ones and bring harmony.

Keep your objects in place for four hours, then you may remove them. After you have done this, call the relative(s) in question and invite them over for dinner. You will find that they respond positively to you and if later on things get strained, just do the ritual again. It also works for friends.

The home

The home is the centre of a family's universe. It is a place to feel loved, secure and happy. We can all live in houses, but it takes a little magic to make a house a home.

Contrary to popular belief I don't live in a castle, although I would love to. I do live in a small two-bedroomed end terrace which, although small for my growing family, does us just now. I work from home, so I need to be able to function within it on many levels. If your home is in harmony, then you will find that your life is also. On the flip side of this, if your home is in chaos you will find personal stability impossible. From a young age I can remember my gran and mum spring cleaning and placing bundles of sage around the house. I will offer you an insight into some of the rituals my family and I have used for many decades. It is these rituals which make my house a home.

CLEARING YOUR SPACE

Space clearing has become one of the new terms bandied about within the New Age movement over the past couple of years. It is thought to have originally been practised by Native Americans. However, I would say that most cultures have their own form of this ritual. My gran did it all her life and it just came naturally to her as a homemaker.

Space clearing basically means getting a home ready to live in. Any negative and stagnant energy is removed to make way for positive energy. It is a good idea do this whenever you move to a new home or whenever there has been a negative change such as death or illness in the household. Any house I moved to with my family was space cleared before a single piece of furniture was moved in. I also remember that before my mother brought my newborn sisters home she cleaned the house, burned incense and sprinkled salt about. I now know what she was doing, but then I just thought it was a bit of fun.

Space clearing isn't just about physically cleaning and clearing out your home, but is a state of mind too. My gran had a little brass bell she would ring around her house when we visited her on a Sunday. She told me that the sound would break any bad atmosphere which was left behind when relatives had visited. I still have her little bell and I use it to help me with my daily meditation.

By space clearing your home you will create a sanctuary so that when you come in from a tough day you can just kick off your shoes and relax on your sofa.

The best time to spring clean is in spring, of course. This is when the new cycle of life begins, the bulbs begin to grow and baby animals are born. But you can do it at any time. I have devised a simple set of instructions for you. To space clear your home:

⋆ You have to prepare your home.
⋆ You have to prepare your mind and spirit.
⋆ You have to get your tools ready.

Then you are ready to space clear.

Preparing your home

Before you start this process your home must be ready for it. By this I mean that it must be cleaned from top to bottom. All dust must be removed, as this can trap negative stagnant energy. All clutter must be removed as well. Clutter is anything that you don't need and that is just wasting space. So this is a good time to clear out cupboards and wardrobes and get rid of any clothes or objects you no longer need. Well, I never said this space clearing was easy, did I?

Once your home is cleared and clean, you are ready to go on to the next stage.

Preparing yourself

As well as the other tools you will use in this ritual you will also use yourself. In fact you will help to clear the house of its negativity just by the power of your mind. You also have the power to uplift and purify your home, but you need to be ready for this.

To prepare yourself, sit quietly where you won't be disturbed. Try to clear your thoughts of all negativity. Think of positive things such as a day at the beach or a field full of daisies. Feel glad that your home is going to benefit from your ritual. In fact it is going to get a much-needed energy boost. Think of the intentions you have for your home, for example making it happy and harmonious.

Next, one of my favourite subjects: protection. As you are dispelling negativity from your home you need to make sure that it is driven away and that it won't stick to your aura. To do this, sit at peace and close your eyes. Imagine that on the top of your head there is a switch. Once you flick this on, a golden light will cover your whole body and give you protection against negativity.

You should now wash your hands in salty water to cleanse and purify them.

Getting your tools ready

By 'tools' I don't mean your feather duster or beeswax, but objects and elements which help you to space clear. This list is not cast in stone, as you can use whatever feels right to you. I am just telling you what I use, as advised by my gran. In time you will become tuned in to your home and will discover what works best for you.

Sacred sound: Sound is able to bring balance to people, places, even objects. Just think of how relaxed you feel when listening to your favourite music. Sound has been used for space clearing for thousands of years. Primitive tribes in Africa would use rattles and drums to sanctify ground they held religious rites on. Even churches use sound to tune in to a higher spiritual level. At a deeper level, sound creates a physical vibration which can help eliminate negative energy.

You can use any musical instrument to space clear, or you can use a bell, as I do, prayer chimes or even a harmony ball. A harmony ball is one which jingles, as it has little chimes within it. The sound it makes is very refreshing. Find what works for you.

Holy smoke: Over the past four years, as well as using my little bell to space clear, I have used smudging. This is making smoke by burning a bundle of herbs, normally sage. It was my sister Ayfer who first told me about smudging. She discovered it while travelling around North America. When she stayed on a Native American reservation and she witnessed it being used in ceremonies. The smoke purifies the air of the home. Sage is also a protective herb which eliminates negative vibes. As well as smudge sticks you can also use incense, which has the same properties. I would use patchouli to space clear, as it helps bring harmony.

Purifying waters: I remember as a child watching in wonder as the priest came to my house armed with a little black pouch. In it he had a bottle in the shape of Mary the Virgin. He walked around the house sprinkling holy water and praying under his breath. I asked him what he was doing, as I was an inquisitive nine-year-old. He told me that he was purifying the house and stopping evil from working its way in.

In most cultures water is highly revered, not least because it helps us to survive, and holy water will indeed consecrate your home. You can get it from a church, shrine or temple, or even make your own. To do this you need to get water from a natural source, water which has come directly from Mother Nature herself. It can be from a freshwater well or spring and even bottled spring water will do, as long as it states 'bottled at source' on the label. To energise your water, pour it into a ceramic bowl and leave it outdoors on the night of a full moon. In the morning it will be charged with lunar energy. It is then ready to be used in your ceremony.

Sacred salt: Before there was money there was salt. In ancient times it was a valuable commodity, as it was used for food preservation. It was also known to have healing properties and was useful for healing sores and soothing limbs. Salt also deflects negative energy away from your home. This is why you pour salt over your left shoulder if you spill it. The best salt to use for space clearing is natural sea salt or rock salt. Place some carefully ground salt into a bowl ready for use in your ritual.

Now that you have prepared your home, charged yourself and assembled your tools, you are ready to space clear your home.

Method

Step 1: Recheck all your cleaning efforts around the home. Make sure that anything broken is fixed and that any plants are looking well and not wilting. If a plant is on its way out, put it out of its misery and ditch it. Replace it with a happy plant. Then make sure you have washed your hands.

Step 2: Place fresh flowers around your home to bring a sense of well-being and colour to it.

Step 3: Make sure all pets are out of the home, as they can carry stagnant energy.

Step 4: Put all your tools on a tray or large plate. This makes it easy for you to carry them from room to room.

Step 5: Decide which room you are going to start in and take the tray in there. Stand in the room and allow your energy to flow. Know that you have the knowledge and power to clear the space.

Step 6: Take the instrument for sound first. Walk around the room in a clockwise direction, making the sound as you do so. Make sure the corners are not missed out, as these can harbour stale air.

Step 7: Then take your smudge stick or incense. As you light it, think about the smoke filling every space in the room, neutralising it and purifying your space. Again walk in a clockwise direction, allowing the room to be filled with healing smoke.

Step 8: It is now the turn of your holy water. This should be sprinkled around the room. Again, make sure you don't miss the corners.

Step 9: Your sacred salt can now be sprinkled around the room, just as you would with a carpet freshener. Then leave the bowl in the centre of the room for three minutes.

Carry this out in each room and at the end say a blessing for the help you have had from your own divine source. You should feel the spirit of the house lift.

I always suggest that once you have finished you

cleanse yourself in a nice hot bath with lovely oils in it. My favourites are camomile and lavender.

You can carry out this ritual in spring or whenever you feel your home is harbouring negativity. Afterwards your home will be full of harmony and happiness.

CHAPTER 7
Enjoy Tip-Top Health

EVERY TIME I DO a reading not only do I see what is going to happen to a person, I also get a sense of their overall well-being. I see their aura, which to me is a visual indication of how they are feeling both physically and mentally. The aura is a funny old thing and not all psychics can see it. There are many explanations as to what it is, but the simplest is that it is the spiritual covering we all have around our bodies. If we get sick, it changes colour and if it is torn, this can also reflect injury or hurt.

I remember once reading for a lady who looked happy and positive, but her aura was showing me that within her body was a ticking time bomb as yet unseen. Not to frighten her, I explained that I could see a visit to the doctor being on the cards and that the 'well woman' clinic would be significant. Sure enough, she called me four months later to let me know that she went to the clinic and was found to have an abnormal smear. After further investigation it was revealed she had cervical cancer. Luckily it was caught in time.

As a psychic I have a responsibility not to frighten people when they come to me for advice. My gran instilled this in me. She would say, 'Tell people what is of use to them that day, not what will prey on their minds for the rest of their lives.' So if I see illness I will speak about it only if I can be positive about it and help the person to deal with it.

In order to do my work, it is so important that I am balanced at all times. I can't read if I feel unwell or emotionally drained. In this chapter I will show you how to live a holistic life, as I do, so that you can be happy and healthy from the inside out. Then you will be able to develop your psychic senses even more, as you will be feeling great – and looking great too, as we will also take a look at some old beauty remedies, from skin tonics to hair rinses. I am not going to preach to you, as I am a big girl, always have been, and I do enjoy the good things in life, like a great meal with tasty wine. But I do walk the walk and talk the talk, as I exercise regularly and eat a healthy vegetarian diet – even if a wee bit too much sometimes.

I have put together a five-point plan for you to boost your well-being. Start by just doing what you can: there is no pressure. In time you will find that you can do it all and you will be well on the road to feeling great inside and out.

RUTH THE TRUTH'S WELL-BEING PLAN

1. *Increase your energy*: Isn't it a drag when you feel tired and sluggish all the time? To increase your energy levels you need to improve your diet and exercise more. To improve your diet you need to eat a balanced array of foods and cut down on fats and refined sugar. I also try to eat as many raw vegetables as possible, as these are packed with vital vitamins. Water is also important as it flushes out toxins and keeps you hydrated. I drink at least five glasses a day. You also need to ensure that your diet is sufficient in iron, as a deficiency can cause you to feel exhausted all the time. Good sources of iron are lentils, soya and broccoli. Enjoy a healthy stomach also with a pot of live yoghurt each day. Having a healthy digestive system will ensure you are working physically to your full potential.

Once you are eating right you will feel better, but exercise is key to all of this. I go on long walks with the kids, swim at least twice a week and also enjoy aqua fit. My main love is dancing – Latin American dance is my passion and it keeps me fit. You can choose to do whatever form of exercise you want. Just be easy on yourself at the start and always take medical advice first, just to be on the safe side.

Improving your diet and taking exercise will keep your energy levels at a decent level.

2. *Tackle stress head on:* I hate being under stress. It does happen to me sometimes when I let things get on top of me, but in general I have learned to handle it. Stress is basically a primitive response to factors which cause us to feel out of control or in crisis. It can have a positive effect, as the rush of the hormone adrenaline can give us a short energy boost, which is useful for sportspeople, but not for the normal Joe Bloggs, which is most of us.

You will know that you are suffering from stress if you are finding it difficult to concentrate and you are irritable and/or have headaches. You can also find that you change your outlook on life or have palpitations, which I get myself. As a psychic, you find that stress can really muck up your line of thought, and if you are learning to develop your skills it can affect your progress.

The first thing I want you to do is think about all your stress factors. Take a piece of paper and write down whatever is causing you stress. Examples of mine would be taking on work I have no time for and the kids being sick but still having to make a deadline.

Once you have written down your stress factors, look at them and think about ways in which you can alleviate them. For example I get stressed by taking on too much work and I could solve this by learning to say no. You have the power to make a difference in your life, so think about how to do it. Try following the strategy below to handle stress more effectively.

How to handle stress

☆ Organise your workload: If you are stressed by your work, look at what you have to do and learn to delegate. Then prioritise all the tasks you have left. Take regular breaks during your day and have a cup of refreshing herbal tea or even take a walk to clear your head. If you don't work from home, make it a work-free zone. Try not to bring work home at all, or else do it all on the train before you get to your front door. If do you work from home, as I do, make sure you set clear boundaries of when you are working and when you are not. Juggling work and children can be difficult and childcare is my biggest stress. If your child is at school or nursery, make sure you have a back-up plan if they are sick or off school.

☆ Be assertive: So many people write to me stressed out of their nut because they just can't say no. So often we take on extra work or family duties just to please others. Next time you are asked to do something you have no time for, say no. Be firm and concise and you will feel elated!

☆ Eat properly: Some foods have been found to aggravate stress levels and response, in particular stimulants such as alcohol and caffeine. Sure, they give you an initial high, but this soon wears off, leaving you tired and sluggish. So instead drink herbal teas or fruit infusions. If you don't like these, then water or fruit juice will also do the trick. Vitamin C has been found to combat stress levels by reducing stress hormones found in the blood. Eating plenty of fresh fruit and veg will ensure you get the vitamin C you need.

★ Take exercise: Exercise not only helps increase your energy levels but also reduces stress. Make time for a little exercise every other day – 30 minutes for maximum benefit.

Once you have dealt with your stress you will feel better and more in control of your life.

3. Become a Sleeping Beauty: Anyone who knows me well will tell you how much I love my sleep. If I don't get at least eight hours a night I am like a real bear with a sore head. I also often take a short afternoon nap, just to give myself a wee rest during the day. In fact my family always make a joke of this as I am often away for a nap when they try to call me. We all need sleep to live. If we don't have it we can become irritable, tired, depressed and prone to illness. While we sleep our body undergoes many amazing processes such as cell regeneration and body relaxation. Also, we dream while asleep and this is an important factor when you are trying to develop psychic or intuitive ability. After all, many of your dreams will be giving you indications of what is coming to you and/or messages from the spirit world and beyond. More on this later.

How much sleep you need differs from person to person. For example I can't function without at least eight hours a night, but my husband can do OK with only five. Whatever is right for you, for this part of your holistic overhaul you need to put a good sleep management plan into practice. Then you will find sleep easier to maintain and you will get more out of it.

Sleep management plan

★ Make your bedroom a relaxing haven. It should only be used for sleep and relaxation but if you must work in it, as I do, get a screen to hide your equipment when you are not working. Choose relaxing colours for your room, such as lilac or cream, and have soft lighting.

★ Before going to bed don't eat anything too heavy, as this raises your metabolic rate and will in turn bring a restless night's sleep. It is also best not to take coffee or tea before going to bed, as these stimulants can cause you to be too awake before bedtime. You could have a milky drink or a herbal tea to settle you down for the night.

★ Another good idea is to have a nice bath with aromatherapy oils or herbs just before bed. I make up a muslin pouch of dried lavender, camomile and a couple of drops of sandalwood oil, then I just tie it up and pop it in a running bath to infuse it. I always find this very relaxing.

★ To help me sleep I always place a couple of drops of lavender oil on my pillow. I find this just gives me a nice drowsy feeling and I soon drift off and start snoring like a pig. Well, my husband tells me so!

With this easy-to-follow plan you should find that you are getting all the sleep you need.

4. Become a Happy Chappy: Laughter has been found to lower levels of the stress hormone cortisol and it also helps to elevate the mind and keep you on an even keel. I love a good laugh. In fact I find it hard to take things too seriously, and this includes myself. When my friend Anna was ill with cancer we used to be in stitches laughing at the most stupid of things, to the point that we were often in tears. This continued even when Anna was slipping away from us. Her sister Kathryn and I never once stopped the fun. I must admit that people often thought we were a bit mad, but that is what Anna would have wanted.

If you look at serious people, they tend to have tense faces, bad posture and above all more wrinkles. So learn to clear your mind of negative thoughts, low self-esteem and anger. In their place put happy thoughts, love and creativity. Think about the last time you had a great blast. Harness this feeling and bring it into your life on a daily basis.

How to harness the fun in your life

☆ Get on the phone or e-mail a friend who makes you laugh. In no time at all you will have a smile on your face.

☆ Read a funny book. One of my favourites is *Bridget Jones's Diary*. Every time I read it, I go into a spasm of laughter.

☆ Catch a comedy on video or the telly. I love TV and find comedies keep me sane even at sad times. I have a videotape of the *Chewing the Fat* comedy series from BBC Scotland. By the time I have watched this I find my troubles aren't half as bad as I thought they were.

☆ Do something you really enjoy. For example one of my favourite things is going out for a meal with friends. I often find that listening to others and enjoying good food helps me to put my life into perspective.

If you can be happy, then you will discover your life really does improve – and then you will have even more to be happy about!

5. Harness your creativity: Creativity is one of the most important skills you need when you are developing your psychic ability. Without it we would have no 'cosmic flow', as I call it. For example when my gran was reading the tea leaves, she would close her eyes and imagine what the symbols meant. She would conjure up sights and sounds and relay these to the person she was doing the reading for. Her imagination made the symbols in the tea leaves move and mean something. Without creativity this just wouldn't have been possible.

Being creative doesn't just mean that you are good at art, but that you have flair in many areas, from music to art to design, and so on. In fact, every thought we have comes from a creative process, no matter what it is about. So you are already being creative without even thinking about it. But how can you develop your creative side? My simple guide will show you how.

How to tune in to your creative side

Practising imagery work will help you to develop your creative response. This means that you will be able to just call it up whenever you want.

☆ Start by lying down on a comfortable bed when you know you won't be disturbed for at least 20 minutes. Close your eyes and breathe deeply, listening to each breath. At the same time move your arms above your head nice and slowly. Stretch from your fingertips to your toes in a long line. Imagine you are being stretched tall and lean. Repeat this twice and you will feel nice and relaxed.

☆ Next imagine that you are walking along a beautiful golden shoreline. The sea is calm and lapping up in small white waves. As you walk along, the sand is feeling warm under your bare feet. You feel happy and relaxed and have a big smile on your face. You reach a white bench and decide to sit there for a while. You watch the sea and smell its freshness. All is well in your world.

✭ Once you are feeling good you decide to walk back along the shoreline to the point where you started. Take in the colours all around you, the sky, the water and the sand. Say goodbye to your happy place.

✭ Now return to the present world. Bring your arms back down to your sides and slowly open your eyes.

This practice will help you to build up your imagination for future use.

Enjoy a creative life

✭ Try looking at things from a different perspective. Never view your life as run-of-the-mill, as it can be exciting in every single aspect. For example, when you are doing your shopping in your usual supermarket, decide that you are creating a sense of good nutrition for yourself. If you take a lovely long country walk, decide that you are creating a sense of well-being for yourself. Just viewing yourself differently will allow this to work. It will take time, but that is all the fun of this exercise and you will find that you are never bored again.

✭ Act on your dreams and aspirations. You may want to spend more time taking up a new skill, such as learning a new language, or you could have a desire to learn salsa dancing or pottery. Don't hold back, as this will be a good time to let your aspirations come to fruition.

☆ Learn to express yourself. During the personal development workshops I used to run I would bring along a whole pile of magazines, coloured pens, scissors, glue and poster sheets of paper. This was to allow my students to make up their own poster representing all that they wanted in their lives, all their hopes and dreams and wishes for a brighter future. By doing this they were tapping into their creative side. Most of the posters showed things that they could achieve with a little prompting and personal development.

You can do the same. Look at magazines and if you see a picture which triggers something in your mind, just cut it out. This is a very therapeutic exercise and I still do it sometimes when I need focus in my life. Expressing yourself in this way will help you to look at life from a fresh new angle.

By now your creativity will have developed to the point where all your senses, including your sixth sense, will be more effective.

Natural beauty

There are many ways of looking good and beauty doesn't have to cost the Earth. Here are a few helpful hints on how to keep your hair healthy and your skin looking great. Nothing I will mention will cost a lot of money, as most of my tips come from my grannie, who was never wealthy in cash terms.

I thought I would start with your hair. I certainly know that when my hair is unwashed and looking a mess I feel a mess inside and out. One of my childhood memories is the smell of beer in the kitchen. This wasn't due to the fact my mother had a drink problem – far from it, as she is teetotal – but she would steep her hair in beer. You see, my mum had the most beautiful long auburn hair. In fact she could sit on it, it was so long – long and silky. This section will look at ways in which you can keep your hair looking good, and they are all natural.

BRIGHT SHINY HAIR TONIC

I have seriously dyed hair. I can't remember my natural colour, but looking at my roots I guess it is dark brown. Because of all the chemicals used on my hair it can quickly look dry and distressed. To give it a quick pick-up I use a hair tonic my grannie used to swear by.

Put 3 tablespoons of apple cider vinegar into a cup of lukewarm water. Shampoo your hair as normal and use the tonic as a final rinse. Then dry your hair normally.

People often comment on how bright my hair is when I have done this, so it does work and it only costs pennies.

HELPING FLAKY SCALP

From time to time I have a flaky scalp. I find this unsightly and annoying. My Turkish gran had this problem too, as has everyone in our family at different times. In Turkey they swear by parsley for its many miraculous properties. In fact, if used correctly, parsley will mop up dandruff. It works by rebalancing the scalp's acid/alkali ratio.

To try this herbal remedy, take a Pyrex dish and put half a cup of finely chopped fresh parsley in it, then pour about 500 ml (1 pt) of boiling water over it. Let it stand for an hour. Massage the liquid/parsley mix into your scalp and keep it on for 15 minutes. Use a shower cap to keep everything in place for that time. Then simply rinse it out and wash your hair as you would normally. The flaky scalp will be a thing of the past and although this remedy is a little messy, it is well worth it.

NATURAL HAIR LIGHTENER

I have only ever had my hair lightened once and if you had seen it you would know why I will never do it again. The colour was supposed to be a copper red but ended up flamingo pink. I looked like Mrs Slocombe from *Are You Being Served?* My sister Ayfer, however, wanted to be a blonde from the age of eight. Of course at that age my mum refused to let her bleach it. By the time she was 13, though, my gran finally told her of a little trick she used during the war. She would simply put a lemon juice rinse on to her hair, take a book and sit out on a sunny day to let the lightening process work. My sister did this and ended up with lovely natural-looking highlighted hair.

If you want to try this out for yourself, all you need to do is mix 10 tablespoons of lemon juice to a cup of lukewarm water and apply this as a final rinse. Comb it through and then look for some sunshine to dry your hair.

HAIR MAGIC FOR REDHEADS

As I said before, my mum used to have long auburn hair, but even if my hair does look red, unfortunately I am not a natural redhead. One of the dreams I had when I was a little girl was that I would wake up with long red curly hair. Of course this never materialised, but a girl can dream, can't she? For those of you lucky enough to have naturally red hair, this next tonic will leave your hair a vision in red.

Pour 2 cups of boiling water over half a cup of dried marigold flowers and leave it to stand for 30 minutes. Then strain the liquid and after shampooing, rinse your hair with it. Do this in a basin so that you can re-use the rinse. Rinse your hair three times and then let it dry naturally. Marigolds have enzymes and chemicals in them which help to rejuvenate red hair.

HAIR MAGIC FOR BRUNETTES

The best tonic for brunettes is a lavender rinse. This can be made by putting a few drops of essential oil in a cup of lukewarm water. After shampooing, rinse just the once and then let your hair dry naturally.

Alternatively you can make a lavender tea using dried lavender, half a cup to be precise. Put the lavender in a teapot and fill it with boiling water. Let it infuse for 30 minutes, then shampoo your hair and use the rinse as before. Rinse into a basin, because with this one you will need to rinse your hair three times. Afterwards you will find that the lavender's oils have helped to bring out the brown hues of your hair. Your scalp will also feel great.

HAIR MAGIC FOR BLONDES

One of my dearest friends has the most beautiful natural long blonde hair. Her secret is a rinse she heard about on her travels to the Far East. She was finding it difficult to get shampoo and a local of the village she was in told her to make camomile tea and use it to wash her hair. Camomile flowers have long been known for their healing properties, but they are also very good at bringing out the highlights in naturally fair hair. Having found the plant growing by the roadside, my friend went about making a tea. On rinsing her hair with it, she found it had been totally cleaned and conditioned. Since then she has used the rinse once a month and her hair is testament to the positive effect camomile has on blonde hair.

To make a camomile rinse, all you will need is a cup of boiling water and half a cup of camomile, either fresh, dried or in tea bags. Add the water to the camomile and let it brew for an hour. Filter the liquid off and use it as a rinse after you have washed your hair. Again, do this in a basin so you can retrieve the fluid and repeat the rinse three times. Let your hair dry naturally.

NO MORE OILY HAIR

Oily hair plagued me for many of my teenage years. I also had limp greasy hair after both my pregnancies, which made me feel miserable, as there is nothing you can do with it.

My gran was a great believer in many things, none more so than the merits of rosemary. She would often make me a hair rinse with fresh rosemary picked from her wee garden. As soon as my hair had been rinsed with what I called her 'magic potion', it would be bouncy, manageable and above all free from grease. To this day I use this rinse whenever my hair gets all hormonal again.

For this rinse you will require half a cup of fresh rosemary, as dried rosemary doesn't seem to work quite as well, and 2 mugs of water in a pot which has a lid. Put the rosemary into the pot with the water and put it on a medium heat. Once it comes to the boil, let it simmer on a low heat for 15 minutes. The smell is wonderful and if you have the suspicion of a cold, it will clear your sinuses. Once 15 minutes have passed, cover it and let it stand for 24 hours. Strain and bottle it, and keep it in the fridge until you are ready to use it. Use it three times as a rinse and you will find it dries your hair up wonderfully. Use it once a month to keep grease at bay.

'A beautiful skin shows there is beauty within'

When your skin looks good you feel good inside. For some of us it may be OK to put on make-up to hide our flaws, but this is not the case for everyone. As someone who has had problem skin in the past I know how soul-destroying that can be. Luckily I had a family full of old remedies to help me through the worst of times. In addition I have collected many natural remedies from all over the world.

What I am going to show you will be simple to make and won't cost the Earth. Once I have finished with you, you'll be looking absolutely fabulous! I used to run workshops called 'Beauty from your Larder'. Read on and you'll find out why.

BEAUTIFUL SKIN REGIME

I have always been a great believer in the old adage 'cleanse, tone, moisturise'. I do this faithfully at least once at day and for someone in their thirties I reckon my skin is looking good. You can go to any shop and buy cleanser, toner and moisturiser or you could just follow my herbal remedies. You'll find the ingredients either in your kitchen or your bathroom.

Cleanser

My grannie had the most beautiful skin and my great grannie on my grandad's side was famed for her youthful rosy complexion. Both these ladies cleansed their skin daily with floral water. I always knew this as my grannie's 'special water'. Her medicine was her whisky, but that is a whole different section!

To make this great cleanser all you need is a small bottle of still mineral water and 4 drops of lavender oil and 4 drops of geranium oil. Mix these all together, then clean your face with the special water and cotton wool. Your skin will tingle and you should see all the muck coming straight off.

Toner

The best toner I know of is this one my mum used to make. She heard about it from a farmer's wife she once befriended when she worked in the Highlands. It is great for toning the skin and is especially good if you have spots or a high facial colour.

This time the magic ingredient is mint. Take a cupful of freshly chopped mint, put it in a teapot and fill it with newly boiled water. Let this infuse into a strong mint tea. Then strain away the mint and pop the liquid into a bottle. Refrigerate it before use. You will find your skin automatically tightens up after you use this one.

Moisturiser

This moisturiser has served my family and me well for years. It is easy and cheap but just as effective as some of the expensive brands you can buy. It also helps to keep wrinkles at bay, so we can call this one an anti-ageing cream too. A great aunt of mine discovered it quite by chance during the war when she had run out of face cream and she gave the recipe to me. My mum uses it as well and you should see her skin. For a sixty-something, she looks great.

What you need is a plain lotion or moisturiser with no fragrance. Add 2 drops of lavender oil to it and mix using a spoon. Hey presto, you have a great moisturiser! The anti-ageing properties come from the fact that lavender oil has rejuvenating properties and helps the skin's elasticity.

So you now have a plain and simple beauty regime. But what if you are having problems with your skin? Well, I have some remedies which may be just up your street.

OLD REMEDIES FOR SKIN CONDITIONS

Chapped skin

I do a lot of gardening throughout the year and so my hands can become prone to chapping. I have found that steeping them in a basin full of warm water and 4 camomile tea bags will relieve this problem. I normally do this after my gardening just to ward off any chapping, letting my hands steep for about 10 minutes. This is not only relaxing, but therapeutic also.

Eczema

Both my children have had this awful skin condition at some time or other. To give them instant relief I use one of my gran's sure-fire cures – I peel a potato, grate it and put it on the itchy area in the form of a poultice. This brings instant coolness and even though it sounds a bit mad, the natural juice of the potato helps relieve the inflammation.

Psoriasis

Psoriasis is another sore and unsightly skin condition. I have known sufferers to pay hundreds of pounds for creams and lotions which don't work. Fortunately, aloe vera juice rubbed on to the skin will alleviate these symptoms. If used regularly it can help to clear the condition up totally. You can purchase aloe vera juice or you can use the juice from a leaf of a plant. Either way you will find that this helps. Aloe vera is one of nature's miracles and it helps with so many ailments.

Burns

At one time I used to rent a room from an aromatherapist so that I could do personal readings. One evening I stupidly burned my hand with a candle and ran about the room like a mad woman. The aromatherapist heard the commotion and came in. On seeing what had happened, she put neat lavender oil on the burn. It took away the soreness and within a couple of days it had healed completely. As well as lavender oil, you can use aloe vera gel, which also cools and soothes.

Acne treatment

Not only did I have greasy hair as a teenager, but I also had acne, which made me very shy and withdrawn at times. I tried all of the doctor's medicines, but none seemed to tackle the problem for any length of time. As usual my gran came to the rescue with an old herbal remedy of her mother's.

This remedy is simple. Get a good handful of fresh thyme and steep it in a bowl of boiled water for 30 minutes. Strain the liquid off, bottle and then refrigerate.

As a teenager I used this as a facial rinse for a week and it helped to clear my face up. Afterwards if any spots reared their ugly heads again I just made up a fresh bottle.

By now you should be looking and feeling fantastic. Your face and skin should be a real picture! In fact, being psychic, I can see just how good you look. And if you look good, you are going to feel good too.

CHAPTER 8

Financial and Career Success

ONCE YOU HAVE READ this book I feel that this is one of the chapters you will keep coming back to. The reason I am sure about this is that in the seven years that I have been helping people professionally with my skills they always ask, 'Will I ever come into money?' If I had a pound for every time this was said to me I would be a very rich lady.

A career is also an important part of life. It helps to shape the person and therefore it is so important to do something that you enjoy. My success has been slow and steady. Self-belief has a lot to do with it. This is especially true when you are constantly tested and questioned on your skills. I have had to develop a very tough persona to deal with this part of my job. There have been times when I have been sitting in a television studio listening to people spouting utter rubbish and just wishing I could be relaxing with the kids.

The first part of this chapter is all about personal development, because once you have worked on yourself you will be able to carry out the work involved in building up a successful career or good finances. I am a complete convert regarding personal development. In fact my husband would say that I am a self-help junkie.

This all began when I was 25 and had just had my first child. I had a very traumatic pregnancy and an even worse birth, and on top of this, the PhD I had been studying for had crashed around me. I found myself without a career, with a baby and feeling very ill. I lay in my hospital bed feeling very sorry for myself but amazed by the beautiful child I had brought into the world.

My mother came visiting laden with flowers, fruit and a small book. Unknown to me, she had noticed how down I was. The book was a blessing, as it taught me that for every negative situation there is a positive one waiting to take over. It just depends on how you perceive the situation. As I explained earlier, I turned my negative situation around by starting a personal development column with the *Glasgow Evening Times* and working as a counsellor, helping people with all sorts of problems. I have now beaten post-natal depression twice and got over health scares all because of the power of positive thinking. I can't promise anything, but if you really believe in it, it can make a difference.

Personal growth

First of all I want you to take a good long hard look at yourself. Get a mirror and look at your reflection for two minutes. I know this will be hard, as I hate mirrors myself, but it will serve one very important purpose: it will give you the chance to realise what you are today. Once you have done this, think about what you will look like in the future – in two, five or even ten years' time. Do you like what you see? Or can you make improvements right now?

Now ask yourself whether you are happy with your life, career or financial position. If the answer is 'no' to any of these, then you can learn here how to kickstart your life for the better.

I once read for an old lady of 87. She had always worked as a seamstress and was married with five children. She had spent all her married life being abused by her husband and she dearly wished she could have changed her life for the better. Alas, she never did and it was harrowing to see a life ruined like that. Don't allow the same to happen to you. You can make a difference to your life right now.

GUIDANCE EXERCISE

Answer the following questions truthfully.

1. What three positive words describe your life just now?

2. What three negative words describe your life just now?

3. You have a genie who can grant three wishes just for you. What do you wish for?

4. What three improvements can you make to your life right now?

5. What three things make you happy?

Look at your answers to these questions. They will show you what makes you tick, what makes you sick and what you are aiming for in your life.

Accept that you have the power to change your life. And if you know what direction you are heading in, it will be easier to reach your destination.

The following are some common statements that people come up with when they are working on ways to improve their problems:

'I hate being single or lonely.'
You don't have to be single or lonely. You need to:
    ★ Get a social life.

★ Learn a new skill that gets you out meeting new people.

★ Learn to love yourself first and reinvent a happy new you.

★ Start to smile and look at things in a positive light.

'I allow people around me to treat me badly.'
So many of us just let people treat us like dirt without even complaining. Learn how to:

★ Be assertive and refuse to do anything you don't want to do.

★ Think about times when you have been treated badly and about how you would stop them from occurring now.

★ Every day say: 'I am a strong person who will not accept being treated as second best.'

'I don't feel that I count.'
Low self-esteem will leave you unable to express who you are. Try the following:

★ We all have good qualities. What are three of yours?

★ Name your proudest moment so far and tap into how it felt.

★ Walk tall and dress to impress. You will ooze confidence.

Feeling good about yourself is a state of mind and it can be programmed into you if you let it. Just start off small and work at your personal development one day at a time.

SOLAR POWER HAPPY PERSON RITUAL

I discovered this personal growth ritual a number of years ago when I was writing an article for a magazine. For my research I had to read an old book on Celtic folklore and this was in it. I use it when I am feeling a little bit down and listless. It is my feel-good ritual. The Celtic tribes were very in tune with the planet and its beauty. They used the seasons and the sun to work their magic and this ritual is said to harness the power of the sun. It gives us healing energy and positive rays of hope.

You will need:
★ a piece of gold or yellow material which is big
enough to sit on comfortably
★ fabric paint pens in black and gold
★ 2 yellow candles
★ a bottle of St John's Wort oil
★ a bunch of yellow or orange flowers

Method

The first thing you need to do is to paint a sun on your material to put your personal imprint on it. I designed a symbol of the sun with a happy face and fantastic rays which radiate across the whole material. It is up to you what you do – you can do anything, just as long as it feels right. Then sign your name with black fabric pen at the bottom of the painting and let the material dry.

Carry the ritual out in the room in your house which gets the most sun. The best time to do it is 2 p.m. Sit on the material and imagine that it is a magic carpet full of positive healing energy. Then anoint the candles with the St John's Wort oil (massage the oil into them). Light the candles and place them at the side of the material just in front of you. Be careful that you don't burn yourself or set fire to the cloth. Lift the flowers up and ask Mother Nature to accept them as gifts in return for solar energy. You can say: *'Guiding solar light, make me feel all right.'* Then sit calmly at peace with your eyes closed, feel the sun's glory and know you will be re-energised.

I have done this ritual when I am feeling really awful and it always helps me feel great again. I am sure you will enjoy it too.

Career success

We spend so many hours of our lives working that the least we can do is enjoy it. Can you imagine doing a job you hate for the rest of your life? I hope not, as this would be sad indeed. For career success you need to know what type of work is best for your type of personality. In this section, using my personally selected rituals, career development wisdom and common sense, I will help you to decide what job is right for you. So if you are currently having career difficulties, don't despair. Can you change your path, as I did when I was 25? If you had asked me at 21 what I would be doing at 32 I would probably have said I would be working as a research scientist. I really didn't imagine that I would be sitting here writing this book for you. And whatever your career problems, I have a magical and common sense solution.

FINDING THE RIGHT CAREER

For this exercise you need to know yourself. You need to look at the skills you have just now and the ones you know you could develop. Look at the following list of skills and tick whatever is true of you.

Mind skills:
good at problem solving
can concentrate easily
great memory
clever
conscientious

Coping skills:
can stay cool during crisis situations
calm temperament
able to see a crisis as an opportunity

Office/Administration skills:
computer literate
great organiser
very resourceful

People skills:
great listener
can be assertive when dealing with difficult people
able to make each individual feel special
not embarrassed when talking to new people

Practical skills:
good at DIY
green fingers in the garden
good at sport
enjoy the outdoors

Creativity skills:
good at art and crafts
excellent at designing things
great imagination
flair for writing

Now that you have done this exercise I want you to take a look at your range of skills. Do they fit the job you are doing? If not, then it may be time to do something different. For example, if you work in an office looking at four walls all day and you ticked all of the practical skills and people skills boxes, then maybe you should be considering a career in nursing.

This is only a guide, but I hope that it will help you to realise just how special you are and that you can do other jobs. I wouldn't expect you to give up a good job for something risky, as that is just not practical, but if you are unhappy in your work this exercise may stir your thoughts as to what you might be doing instead. In time you may be able to make these changes happen.

I will speak more about dreams in the next chapter, but for now I want you to take a look at a ritual you can do to discover what your dream job might be.

DISCOVER YOUR DREAM JOB

This is a great ritual for anyone who is undecided about which career they should take up. It should be carried out on a night when the moon is full and clearly visible in the sky.

You will need:
★ 2 blue candles
★ lavender oil
★ a ceramic bowl
★ clear spring water (bottled water will do)

Method

Stand at a window from which you can see the full moon. Light the two blue candles and pour the water into the bowl. Add 4 drops of the lavender oil. Then take the first candle and allow the wax to fall into the water. Do this with the second candle also. Then repeat twice: *'Full fat moon, let me dream of the job I should do soon.'* Then go to your bed and sleep.

In the morning when you wake, quickly make a note of any dreams you have had before they go out of your head. Then take a look at the bowl. See whether the wax has formed any shapes you can recognise and interpret. For example, seeing books may mean you go ahead and become a teacher. Use your imagination to interpret what you see.

When I did this, I was 17 and I dreamed that I was flying on an aeroplane. I had to get my mum to decipher what the wax was saying, as it was difficult. Finally she pointed out a person looking at a crystal ball. The flying was related to the psychic abilities which I now use in my work and the crystal ball is self-explanatory now, but then I thought it had got it wrong, as science was my thing.

Enjoy this little ritual. You will have a lot of fun with it.

Working with other people

If you find yourself in a job you don't like for whatever reason but you can't leave it, then there are some practical things you can do to improve the situation. A lot of us feel overworked, underpaid and abused, but it doesn't have to stay this way, so read on.

One of our main stresses at work stems from the fact we have to work with other people. Sometimes this can be difficult. In many cases communication is a big problem. Say you are at the end of your tether as you are overworked, but the best person to speak to about this is your boss and you don't get on with him or her. In that case you have another problem right away. If you are finding communication difficult, why not try out this little ritual my gran taught me?

HAPPY MEETING RITUAL

If you are meeting a boss or work colleague you find it difficult to communicate with, do this the day before the meeting at 7 p.m.

You will need:
★ 2 white candles
★ 1 purple ribbon
★ a bunch of sweet-smelling flowers such as
freesias or honeysuckle
★ pen and paper

Method

The night before your meeting, light your candles. Write the person's name on the paper and them roll it up like a scroll and tie it with the ribbon to keep it from unrolling.

Offer the sweet-smelling flowers as a peace offering and say: *'Make my meeting flow with good speak. Allow the result to be positive within the week.'* Then close your eyes and imagine that you are at the meeting and that it is going well. People are talking and there is good communication in general.

After this ritual the meeting may well go as you imagine. I do this before any meetings I am a little bit worried about.

Finding work stressful

I say here 'finding work stressful', but it is both what life throws at you as well as the added stress of keeping a job that can get a bit much. I find my stress levels can be on the rise for much of my working week if I don't keep on top of things. The worst time of the day for me is the morning, when I have to dress and feed the children and take them to school and nursery. All I need is Thomas throwing a wobbly because of what he has to wear and Jessica not wanting her breakfast, and I feel my stress levels soar. You will now know that having high stress levels most of the time is bad for your health. You need to take action. If you do, you will find your work easier to handle.

RUTH THE TRUTH'S STRESS TEST

The first thing I want you to do is to take my stress test to see how stressed you are. Look at the effects of stress listed below and tick which ones you are suffering from just now.

Psychological effects:
anxiety
anger
depression
guilt
hurt
obsession
embarrassment
tension
lack of enthusiasm
cynicism
helplessness
reduced self-esteem
worry
mood swings
withdrawal
lack of concentration
nightmares
suicidal thoughts
paranoia

Physiological effects:
palpitations
indigestion
low immunity
diarrhoea
weight loss/gain
backache
neckache

excessive sweating
breathlessness
nausea
tightness in the chest
tiredness
rashes/skin problems
twitches
clenching the jaw/fist
muscle aches
menstruation changes
headaches/migraines

Behavioural effects:
poor time-keeping
moodiness
increase in alcohol drinking
compulsive behaviour
talking fast
walking fast
eating fast
change of sleeping pattern
loss of libido
change of appetite
waking up early and not being able to go back to sleep
increase in coffee drinking
poor quality of work
increase in smoking
taking drugs
increase in accidents

irritability
slurred speech
being off work more due to illness

Now look at how many you have ticked.

☆ If you have ticked less than 5 overall then you are handling your stress levels well.

☆ If you ticked 5–10 then you need some stress management.

☆ If you ticked more than 10 then you must act now, as stress is seriously affecting your health and life.

HOW TO COMBAT STRESS

Stress makes you feel ill. I should know: I have suffered from it for many years on and off. I am getting better at dealing with it now. I make sure I have time to take relaxing baths and chill out with a glass of wine and a glossy magazine. Here are my top five ways of tackling stress head on:

1. *Exercise:* Exercise releases stress and increases endorphins, which are chemicals in the blood that make you feel good. Exercise also keeps you alert and full of beans. It is recommended that you do 30 minutes of exercise every other day for a healthy lifestyle. You can go walking, jogging, cycling or swimming – anything you enjoy. I like swimming and light aerobics to keep stress at bay.

2. *Aromatherapy:* I am a firm believer in the healing powers of aromatherapy. My gran used to have hankies scented with lavender oil for headaches long before aromatherapy was ever popular. For beating stress I would suggest you take a relaxing bath with camomile and lavender oils. Just lie back and feel good about life. I tend to close my eyes and just let my mind drift. Even when you're at work you could have an oil burner or one of these new-fangled vaporisers. Use a mix of rosemary, lavender and sandalwood oils for a relaxing working atmosphere.

3. *Colour therapy:* Colour is all around us and it has an effect on every aspect of our lives, whether we know it or not. Studies in prisons showed that when clinical white walls were painted a cool blue there was less violent behaviour. If you work in an office, try to have paintings or posters on the walls which have purple-blue hues in them. This will help you stay calm even in the most stressful times.

4. *Prioritise:* This is something that we should all learn to do. I am sure that at some time or other you have found yourself overwhelmed by a great a pile of things to do. Your work needs to be ordered so that the most pressing things are done first and so on right down to things which can wait or, better still, be passed on to someone else. Doing this will give you a feeling of control.

5. Kick the habit: If you smoke, drink coffee or alcohol or use drugs then you will be making your stress symptoms worse, not better. If you are under stress, you need to avoid any major stimulants. This will help you cope with your stress, not just run away from it. I always remember a woman I worked with who had to have at least three cups of strong coffee in the morning before she could work. On this particular day the kettle was broken and she couldn't have her coffee. Within 10 minutes she was shaking and crying. She was totally addicted to caffeine and it put me off for life. You will find you do better with herbal teas, fruit juice or, if you have to, tea in moderation.

Once you have taken on board my five-point plan, you will find that stress is not ruining your life as it did before.

Your work environment

Where you work is just as important as how you work. Wherever you work you can make subtle changes to ensure that your environment is helping you to reach your full potential rather than hinder it. In my office, which also doubles as my bedroom, I have a screen which hides my computer when I am sleeping. I also have an array of specially selected crystals and plants to help me work in harmony with my environment. Here is a list of options you can take to make your working space more effective.

IMPROVING YOUR WORK SPACE

1. Your desk is your own personal space. To be able to think clearly you must keep it free of clutter. Make sure it is clean, organised and well presented. Doing this will make working a pleasure and not a chore.

2. On your desk have an object which reflects your goals. This could be a postcard with a bridge on it reflecting transition and positive movement or a Buddha for peace and harmony in the workplace.

3. If you work at a computer, have an amethyst crystal next to it as this absorbs negative energy. Clear quartz will also help you to have a clear mind.

4. Plants can extract any pollutants from the air of your working space. Peace lilies and mother-in-law's tongues are especially good for this.

5. Your concentration will be enhanced with peppermint and rosemary oil in a dish or on a hanky next to your desk or in the office. The cool aromas circulating will keep you alert for a working day.

With all of this sound advice you should discover a brighter career awaits you. Now to what you really want to know about – money.

Your money

How I wish I had a pound for every time I have been asked 'Will I ever win the lottery?' People often think that by winning money they will be happy, but this is not always the case. I should know, as I have read for some pretty rich people who were having a far from great time. In this section I want you to think about your cash and how you can improve your situation. I will show you the old ways of building abundance in your life and attracting wealth, good luck and prosperity. However, don't be greedy – ask for help to live a better, more positive life.

In Chapter 4 I explained how you could develop your psychic ability to help you in everyday life. Return to that chapter first and refresh your memory, as it is important for you to be in the correct frame of mind when doing money magic. You need to believe that through your thoughts and actions you can make a real difference.

CHARGE YOURSELF UP FOR MONEY MAGIC

This exercise will ground you so that you can work with the natural elements of the Earth.

Step 1: Sit on the floor so that you are nice and comfortable. Drape a green cloth around yourself as a cape and hold a piece of green crystal. You could use aventurine, jade or peridot.

Step 2: Close your eyes and think about how positive your life would be if you were financially secure.

Step 3: Finally, after a few minutes, still with your eyes closed, imagine a beautiful oak tree in full leaf in all its glory.

Step 4: Open your eyes.

Now that you are tuned in to your Higher Self and guides, I want you to think about what you really need. How much money do you need to make a difference to your life? What is your reason for asking for the cash? Who will benefit from it?

Once you have asked these questions you are ready to take the next step.

LUCKY NUMBERS

Sit in peace and quiet and think of numbers. As they pop into your head, write them down. Pick five numbers. These will be your lucky ones for raffles, the lottery and any other number games. If you need bigger numbers, multiply the small ones by 4. This will keep the magic alive.

Take your numbers and write them in gold pen on a

piece of green card. Cut them out and put them into a green pouch to keep them activated with positive energy.

ABUNDANCE RITUAL

I have carried out this ritual whenever times have been difficult for me financially. One particular time I remember doing readings on a tough housing estate. At the end of the sessions I gave out my box for my money to be placed in it. When I checked it, there was 1p in it. I went back and was verbally abused. I had been doing the readings to pay a gas bill as otherwise we were going to be cut off. I went home and did this ritual, which my gran taught me when I was 16. By the end of the week I was sent a cheque for £65 for overpayment of the electricity bill. This was the exact amount I owed the gas.

I can't promise anything, but try it out for yourself.

You will need:
✫ a green candle
✫ rosemary oil
✫ a silver-coloured candlestick
✫ paper
✫ a gold ink pen
✫ a heatproof dish

Method

Carry this out on a Thursday, which is the best day for working money magic. It should be done at 7 p.m. on a waxing moon (one which is building up to a full moon).

Take the candle and anoint it with the rosemary oil. Light the candle and concentrate on the amount of cash you would need to help you out. Take the paper and write this amount down in the gold pen. Then say: *'Money, come to me. It will help me out naturally.'*

Next take the paper and burn it using the flame from the candle. Place it in the heatproof dish and then take the ash which is left and sprinkle it outside in your garden, windowbox or any other place where natural things are growing.

See what happens, but remember to let people benefit from your abundance.

ATTRACTING LUCK TO YOU

If you have been at a low ebb and feel that the world is against you, then it is time to clear this junk from your mind and be positive. A lot of this is just about changing your mindset. If you feel lucky, you are lucky. I have a list here of five things you can do to get lucky:

1. Make sure that in your home all the plugs are kept in the sink and bath, as this keeps your luck from running away from you.

2. Don't have the lid of your toilet up, keep it down, as you could be flushing away your success. Also keep the bathroom/toilet door closed to stop finances from slipping away.

3. Make your own lucky charm to use all the time. First look at the letters of your name. Relate them to the number they correspond to, e.g. A=1, B=2, and so on. Add all the numbers together and the total will be your talismanic lucky number. Scrape this number on to a pebble you have found while out walking. Then place the pebble in a purple pouch. It is now able to keep you lucky.

4. Buy a money plant. I can't stress this enough, as I have two in my living-room window and they do help keep both finances and luck in top form. Make sure the plants are in a sunny position and be gentle on the watering.

5. Keep a small money crystal in your purse or wallet at all times. Choose the stone that relates to your star sign:

Aries: Moonstone
Taurus: Aventurine
Gemini: Rose quartz
Cancer: Citrine quartz
Leo: Amazonite
Virgo: Carnelian
Libra: Agate

Scorpio: Blue sodalite
Sagittarius: Jade
Capricorn: Obsidian
Aquarius: Lapis lazuli
Pisces: Amethyst

Keep these crystals near your cash, lottery tickets or anything you want to attract luck to.

I hope you have enjoyed this chapter and that it brings you some rewards.

CHAPTER 9
The Mystery behind your Dreams

EVER SINCE I was a little girl I have always had the most vivid dreams, but it wasn't until I was about eight that I realised they could be telling me anything of any significance. Around that time I dreamed that a friend of mine was looking into a river and crying uncontrollably. I was really unnerved by this, especially as I was so young at the time. I went to school the next day to discover my friend's little brother had drowned in a freak boating accident. From that day forward I took notice of all my dreams.

My mother's most psychic moments have been through dreams, so it does run in the family. When my mum was in her thirties and we were living in Nottinghamshire she had the most awful nightmare. Even now, 25 years later, she still shakes with emotion when she tells it. She dreamed that a motorcyclist coming home from a night shift skidded on a wet road and crashed into a tree. She could feel the pouring rain and smell the petrol, even hear the sound of the wheels still in motion after the impact. She woke with a start and felt ill the rest of the night. When she got up early the next morning she turned on her radio to discover a motorcyclist had died after losing control on a wet road and hitting a tree. Dreams for my family have always been a window on to other worlds with lessons to learn.

I have always found dreams fascinating and I am sure you will too. Whether you remember your dreams or not, dreaming is something we all do and you can discover the mystery behind your dreams. Where do they come from? What do they mean? How can you interpret them? As we will discover, dream analysis is not as easy as it may first appear. It is an acquired skill. The first rule of thumb is to take into account what is happening to us in our conscious lives, as this will normally have some bearing on what we dream about. Worries will also come to the surface in dreams and turn into real nightmares. Exploring your dreams will also teach you a great deal about yourself. It is for this reason that it should not be taken lightly.

The history of dreams

Since the dawn of time dreams have brought warnings of doom and prophecies of future events. Ancient civilisations considered dreams to be direct communications from the gods, and dream analysis was performed by high priests, shamans and holy men. Each society had its own methods of interpretation. Here I want to take a look at the ancient Egyptians, the ancient Greeks and the Native Americans to see how important dreams were to these cultures. This will give us an idea of how they can be significant to us today.

THE ANCIENT EGYPTIANS

The ancient Egyptians, as far as we know, were the very first people to realise the significance of dreams. They were analysing dreams as far back as 4000 BC, as ancient texts show. The Egyptians' ideas on dreams were simple – they believed in opposites. So if you had a good dream, something bad would happen to you, and vice versa. It was also believed that special messages from the gods would be found in dreams. It was the job of the temple priests to decode the information. They would often sleep in temples to help this process, as they believed that the nearer to their gods they were, the clearer the messages would be.

THE ANCIENT GREEKS

The ancient Greeks were very interested in the whole subject of dreams. They actually developed a system to categorise dreams ready for interpretation.

The oracle dream: This was a dream in which an important figure would reveal what was going to happen. It could also involve gods giving information for interpretation.

The symbolic dream: This was a dream which had many abstract symbols in it, also bright colours and designs. With deep thought the symbols could be analysed to reveal a hidden meaning.

The prophecy dream: This type of dream had a movie-like quality. The characters in the dream were real people and the events really would happen at a later date.

The Greeks were very sophisticated in their dream analysis, as the above indicates, but they also believed that all dreams were important and could in fact heal. Many people would go to temples to try to dream protective and healing dreams which would enrich their lives. For example if a leper dreamed of healing waters cleaning his wounds, he would be understood to have been healed in some way through the power of his dream.

THE NATIVE AMERICANS

The Native North Americans held dreams in high regard, as they believed they were gifts from nature spirits to help in their daily life. The Mohicans would take the message from a dream and then carry out a ritual to complement it. For example, if someone dreamed of a storm they would do a dance to help this happen for the good of their people. They also divided dreams into good and bad dreams and performed rituals to deal with the outcomes.

The Native Americans also used dream catchers. We have all heard of these nowadays. Even my daughter has one above her bed now. The idea was that the web within them would catch the bad dreams but let the good dreams go.

Rituals and dreams went hand in hand in Native American society and many of these rituals are practised to this day. Of course there are far fewer Native Americans now, but it is important for those still around to follow their ancestral roots.

Why do we dream?

It is an amazing fact of life that we spend a third of our time sleeping. In my case it is at least half my time, but that is a different matter! We all need to sleep to recharge our batteries and conserve our energy for another busy day.

Sleep is not a simple process but a highly technical one. I won't bore you with the ins and outs of this; suffice to say that sleep can be divided into separate phases depending on what stage we are at in the process. When we fall asleep first we are in what is called 'slow wave sleep'. This is when our breathing and heart rate slow down. Then after around one to one and a half hours we go into 'REM sleep'. REM stands for 'rapid eye movement'. Our lids quiver as our eyes move about, our heart rate speeds up and our blood pressure rises. It is during this time that we have our most vivid dreams. During the other phases of sleep we do dream, but we don't normally have the ability to recall the dreams.

There have been many studies on the subject of dreaming and there are many theories about why we dream. Here are the most popular:

☆ Dreams help us to face the emotional concerns we have in our waking life.

☆ Dreaming allows us to act out our fantasies and hopes, even if there isn't a chance of them coming true.

☆ Dreams are the brain's way of processing the information it has had to take in over the previous 24 hours.

I also believe our dreams can predict future events, as many of mine have, as have those of people I have met in my line of work.

FORGOTTEN DREAMS

I have at times been in the company of people who have sworn blind that they have never ever dreamed. This is obviously not the case, though I am sure that if you are in the same boat you are screaming at this page right now. We spend at least a quarter of our sleep dreaming, so it will always be difficult to recall all of these dreams. Also, dreams can be muddled and make no sense to man or beast, so often the brain just doesn't process the information. But reading this chapter and picking up my dream tips will help you to recall your dreams as and when you want.

How to interpret your dreams

I truly believe that our dreams are messages, whether they are telling us about our present situation or foretelling what will happen in the future. Ever since I was 13 I have kept a dream journal. It is amazing to look at dreams I had when I was dating my husband as a young 17-year-old and of course my predictive dreams, including those of the Piper Alpha disaster and more recently the Concorde crash. If you want to understand the messages behind your dreams, the best way to start is by keeping a dream journal of your own.

KEEPING A DREAM JOURNAL

For this, all you will need is a hard-backed A4 notebook and a pen. Keep them by your bed each night, with the date already noted at the top of the left-hand page. When you wake up, even if it is during the night, note down on the left-hand side of the notebook all you remember from your dream.

When you wake up properly in the morning, sit by your bed for a couple of moments and close your eyes so that the memories of your dream come flooding back. If you are having trouble recalling your dream, check how you were feeling emotionally and this may well bring back the memories. In time your brain will become tuned in to reliving your dreams.

Once you have been able to describe the most basic segments of a dream you will be able to start filling in any gaps. To do this it is a great idea to break the dream down into different sections. I use 'Theme', 'Setting', 'Symbols', 'Emotions', 'Communications', 'Colour', 'Smell', 'Personal significance' and 'People'. Using these categories you will be able to map out clearly what your dream was about, no matter how bizarre it was.

Theme: What basically happened in your dream?

Setting: Where was the dream set?

Symbols: Were there any shapes or symbols in your dream, for example a cross or a pyramid?

Emotions: How were you feeling during the dream?

Communications: What was said in the course of the

dream? Were there any specific words you can remember as being significant?

Colour: What was the predominant colour of your dream?

Smell: What smells could you detect?

Personal significance: Did the dream mimic your present real-life situation?

People: What people were involved in your dream?

These categories should be written down on the right-hand page of your dream journal. That way you just have to glance over at the left-hand page to see what happened in your dream then fill out the spaces in each section. Within a couple of weeks you will be able to see patterns emerging.

MAKING SENSE OF YOUR DREAMS

Now that you have your dream journal you will have a recording of exactly what you dream about, taking in every aspect of your experience. But how do you make all these words and information mean something to you? At the end of this chapter I present a list of dream symbols and an explanation of common themes. This will help you to make sense of what your dreams are saying to you. For now, however, I want to explain to you how to go about analysing your dreams from the information you gather in your journal.

Remember that although many of our dreams come from a negative situation we are facing, this should be seen as something positive, as it allows us to face our anxieties head on.

The first thing to look at when studying your dreams is any communication that took place in the dream. For example when I was young I dreamed that my dead grandfather came to me and spoke to me in Latin. I didn't know a word of Latin but when what he said was translated it meant something very special to my gran. The words in your dream are like a puzzle. They may not clearly reveal their meaning, but with a closer look and with practice they will yield an important message.

Symbols, too, have great significance and should be noted. This is where a dream dictionary will always come in handy, as it will enable you to look up the meanings of symbols quickly. For example a dream of a tree growing tall and glorious will signify growth and expansion in your life.

You will also be able to analyse your categories. Taking each in turn, ask yourself: 'What does this mean to me and what is my dream trying to tell me?' For example, when looking at setting, if you have noted that your dream was set in a castle this may mean that you don't feel your home is fulfilling its full potential. If you noted that the person most involved in your dream was your mother, it might well be that you are subconsciously worried about her. Look at the other sections to see why that should be. A dream is just like a big puzzle, but if you fit together the pieces slowly and methodically you will be able to build up a picture of what it is all about.

On that note I always feel that you are the best person to analyse your own dreams, as they are personal to you. I once made the mistake of having mine analysed by a psychotherapist who was sure I was mentally unstable. He didn't understand that the images I was seeing in my dreams related to my acute psychic abilities!

CHECKLIST FOR INTERPRETING YOUR DREAMS

To summarise, the way to analyse your dreams is to:

1. Keep an up-to-date dream journal.

2. Relate your dream to all the categories as best you can.

3. Ask of each category: 'What does this mean to me and what is my dream trying to tell me?'

4. Put all the pieces of the puzzle together and, if you need to, use a dream dictionary to help you interpret your dream.

I can promise you that, once you start studying your dreams, interpreting them will become a natural ability which will allow you to understand much more about yourself.

POPULAR DREAM THEMES

This is a great little section that you can use whenever you have had a dream which is quite popular. It will give you a rough idea of what it is trying to tell you. All the following themes are universal, but they will also be personal, as their meaning will relate back to our current situation. As with all dreams, making the meaning fit your own situation is highly important.

I have chosen the most common dream themes: being pursued, falling, flying, teeth falling out, being out in public with no clothes on and finally drowning. I am sure at some time or other you have had a dream involving one of the above scenarios, but what do they all mean?

Being pursued: When you dream of being chased it means that you are running away from a situation you feel trapped by. You need to look at who is chasing you, as they may hold the key to what you are not facing. For example if you are being chased by your boss it could mean you are feeling overwhelmed by the workload they are forcing on you.

Falling: I seem to dream of falling at very crucial periods of my life. It can have a number of meanings, but the most popular is that it relates to a feeling of failure. These dreams are common during divorce or the loss of a job. It is often said that though you are falling you will never hit the floor, as if you do it means that you have died. Of course no one has come back from the dead to tell us if this is true or not.

Flying: This is one of the most pleasant dreams you can have. Dreaming of flying or floating can bring a feeling of euphoria and if you dream this you are often lucid dreaming. This means that you have the ability to control your dream – even if that just means you float to your mate's house to see how they are doing! Dreaming of flying normally means freedom from a particularly restricted element of your life. It also shows that opening up your mind to a wide range of possibilities will be in your favour. For example if you dream of flying on a magic carpet this would signify a desire to travel more than you have done so far.

Teeth falling out: This is one dream I don't recall having, but many people have written to me telling me that they have had this one. To dream of losing your teeth can suggest that you have a real fear of losing power within a very special and close relationship. If the teeth are old and break, then this can be a hint that you are feeling sexually inhibited.

Being out in public with no clothes on: I once had a dream that I was in a well-known department store and as I passed a mirror I saw my reflection and realised I was naked. At that I ran out of the store in a panic! This dream's meaning really depends on how it makes you feel. If you are mortified and want to run for cover, then it can represent the fact you are shy and shun the limelight. If in the dream people just keep going about their normal business as if they don't care, then it can mean that you need to accept yourself warts and all, just as other people are accepting you naked.

Drowning: Water in dreams is thought to signify the subconscious. If you are drowning, it will reflect a feeling of being overwhelmed in a specific part of your life. Your emotions are also important here, as water can symbolise your emotional self at any given time. For you really to understand its significance in a dream it is important to look at the whole picture.

Now from common dreams to common dream symbols. This is a basic guide, but it will help you get to grips with the meaning behind your dreams. If you want to know more I would suggest that you invest in a good dream dictionary.

DREAM SYMBOLS AND THEIR MEANINGS

Animals

Bird: A flying bird represents freedom and a sense of escape. It can also represent the soul and so may have a deep religious meaning. The type of bird is also important. A raven or crow is said to be an omen of death, whereas a dove is a symbol of harmony in life.

Cat: A cat in a dream symbolises femininity and sexuality. Creativity can also be important in this respect.

Dog: A dog represents a faithful friend who will be foremost in your thoughts for one reason or another.

Buildings

Door/Gateway: An open door or gateway can mean a new phase of your life which will be positive for you. If you dream of a closed door or gateway, then you are being held back by something.

House: A house represents the mind. Each room signifies a part of your thinking. For example the bedroom represents the subconscious mind. If it is neat and tidy, then your mind is well organised. On the other hand, if the sitting-room, the conscious part of the mind, is cluttered, it could represent being stressed out in everyday life.

Office: If you dream of an office, especially one you work in, then I am afraid that you are currently bringing your work home with you. If you don't work in an office but dream of one, then you will be dealing with authority soon.

Tower: The tower is a powerful symbol and it tells you to proceed with caution, as being blind to your real situation could cost you dearly.

Important Milestones

Birth: To dream about a birth can mean that a new project is about to get under way. If you are pregnant and you dream of childbirth, it just means that you are anxious about the prospect of having the baby.

Death: Fortunately, to dream of a death normally means that you will soon be hearing about a birth. It can also relate to a sudden change of circumstances.

Wedding: A wedding in a dream is a symbol of unity and solidarity with a given problem. For example you could be involved in a disagreement with a relative but know that to remain united with them would be the best course of action.

Objects

Bed: This symbolises security and well-being, but the condition of the bed is also significant. A tidy bed reveals a secure loving relationship. An unkempt bed can reveal that a relationship is under stress.

Clock: A ticking clock reveals a fear of being overwhelmed by a situation or by work. It can also symbolise repressed emotions which need a release.

Mirror: To look at your face in a broken mirror reveals that you have problems accepting who you are. A clear shining mirror means that you are a vain person who cares more for yourself than others.

Telephone: If the telephone is ringing and goes unanswered then your advice is currently falling on deaf ears and this will leave you frustrated. If the phone is answered, positive news is on its way to you.

Nature

Cave: To dream of a cave means you need to retreat from the outside world as its pace is making you stressed. The cave is seen as a haven where you will find peace and contentment. If it is up high, though, retreating may not be the best way to solve your problems, as friends may be able to help you out instead.

Fire: Seeing a fire in a dream, no matter where it is occurring, means that there is a degree of jealousy in your life. Passion and anger will also be important, depending on the intensity of the flames. Extinguishing a fire shows that you will be able to deal with these emotions effectively.

Flower: To dream of flowers indicates you are seeking inner peace and may well be on the way to getting it. The type of flower is also significant. For example a lily would signify a peaceful period in your life and an orchid a happy sexual experience.

Mountain: If you are at the bottom of the mountain looking up, then you could be feeling you have bitten off more than you can chew in a present situation. On the other hand, if you are climbing the mountain and reach the summit, you will get the success you deserve.

The Sea: Any water in a dream signifies the emotions. A sea is vast and indicates intense feelings. If the sea is calm, then the emotions will not be long-lived. If the sea is very choppy, then these strong emotions will need to be helped with therapy.

People

Angel: To dream of an angel is a very good omen, as it signifies that you are protected by a divine source and that your problems will be solved.

Baby: To dream of a baby represents a new beginning or the birth of a new idea.

Father: He signifies power and authority, but in a way which makes you feel secure, and may also represent your relationship with your father.

Monster: To dream of a monster means that repressed fears and anxieties may need to come to the surface so that you can sort them out.

Mother: She will represent unconditional love and a need to be looked after. If you are the mother in the dream then it is telling you to look after yourself better.

Sex: This is a complicated subject and the meaning is different for every person. What it means in the wider sense is that there is an element of sexual tension in your life.

Places

City: This represents the community as a whole. If it is very busy and sprawling, it could signify that you are feeling confused and overwhelmed by a situation. On the other hand if the city is inviting, with clean streets and quiet roads, it could mean that you are getting your relationships in order.

Island: To find yourself dreaming of an island means you are seeking peace and quiet. It may be you share a house with other people and just need time on your own. Of course the water surrounding the island will signify your emotions, so an island can also mean inner peace.

Stressful Events

Being late for an important meeting: This dream reveals that you are frustrated in an important area of your life.

Exams: If you dream that you are sitting an exam you have not prepared for, it means that you have a fear of failure in a high-profile venture. If, however, you dream of passing an exam, then you will be successful in a venture.

Interviews: To dream of an interview, even one that is going well, reveals that you are under a great deal of stress which is affecting your health and you must do something about it.

Transport

Airport: To dream of an airport reveals that dreams and plans you have had on the back burner may soon materialise.

Car: Are you in the driver's seat? If you are, then you must take control of your life before things go wrong. If someone is driving you, then you may sense that people don't trust you to do things on your own, for example at work.

Car park: A large sprawling concrete car park can represent worries that you may feel are getting out of control. If the car park is full and you can't find a space, then you may feel you are being phased out of an important relationship.

Railway station: If the station is very busy and chaotic, then this could mean that you need to reorganise your life, as it may be out of control.

Road: The type of road is important. A long straight empty road will reveal that a plan you have had might take some time to come together. A crossroads shows this is a time for you to look at your life and see where it is you want to be heading. A winding road with blind bends could be telling you that there is trouble and strife just ahead of you.

I hope you have enjoyed my chapter on dreams and I know that you will find them fascinating. Of course the dream journal is the most important aspect of the chapter, as with this your dreams really will start to speak to you. I know, as I would be lost without mine.

Last Word

I hope you have enjoyed my book. I am sure that it will stand you in good stead to start your new mystic lifestyle. Remember that you are the power behind your spiritual growth, so use your intuition to direct you on your journey. My psychic ability has always enriched my life and I am sure that yours will do the same for you.

Where to Buy

Australian Associations

For those of you living down under, I've gathered some useful addresses for you.

Organic Herb Growers of Australia Inc.
PO Box 6171, South Lismore, NSW 2480; Telephone 02 6622 0100; E-mail <u>admin@organicherbs.org</u>

Organic Retailers' and Growers' Association of Australia (ORGAA)
PO Box 12852, A' Beckett Street, Post Office, Melbourne, VIC 3000; Hotline 1800 356 299
ORGAA is a unique nationwide organisation with a membership consisting of growers, retailers and environmentally aware consumers.

Natural health and beauty

I've listed a range of well known and smaller, family-run businesses for you to contact for natural or organic health products.

Ainsworths
36 New Cavendish Street, London, W1M 7LH; Telephone 020 7935 5330; Fax 020 7486 4313; E-mail ainshom@mfn.com; Website www.ainsworth.com
This chemist can supply you with homeopathic remedies by post.

Aveda
28 Marylebone High Street, London, W1U 4PL; Telephone 020 7224 3157; Website www.aveda.co.uk
Aveda has other branches in London and the UK. They sell organic hair and beauty products.

BiOrganic Hair Therapy
Telepone 0161 872 9813; Fax 0161 872 9848; E-mail sales@biorganics.co.uk; Website www.biorganics.co.uk
This company makes organic hair products for hairdressers, but the goods are available to all by mail order.

Clearly Natural
PO Box 4, Camberley, Surrey, GU15 2YY; Telephone 01276 675609
This small business was the brainchild of Sarah Ropella and provides a complete range of natural vegetable-based and organic toiletries. I use the Provençal breeze soap in my bath, which has lavender to help me relax. As a mail-order company you will find their service swift and thorough.

Dr Hauschka
Unit 19–20, Stockwood Business Park, Stockwood, Nr Redditch, Worcestershire, B96 6FX; Telephone 01527 832863; Mail order 01386 792622; Fax 01386 792623; E-mail enquiries@drhauschka.co.uk; Website www.drhauschka.co.uk

This company makes herbal skincare products from ingredients grown organically (wherever possible). Selected chemists nationwide stock their products.

Earthbound
Telephone: 01597 851157; Website www.earthbound.co.uk
A natural and organic skincare company that makes everything by hand.

The Green People
Brighton Road, Handcross, West Sussex, RH17 68Z; Telephone: 01444 401444; Fax 01444 401011; E-mail organic@greenpeople.co.uk; Website www.greenpeople.co.uk
A mail-order company that makes health products and toiletries with organic ingredients. The products are also available at selected retail outlets.

Jurlique
Willowtree Marina, West Quay Drive, Yeading, Middlesex, U84 9TB; Telephone 020 8841 6644; Fax 020 8841 7557; E-mail info@jurlique.com; Website www.jurlique.com.au
Jurlique makes naturopathic health and beauty products. Call them for stockists.

Neal's Yard Remedies
15 Neal's Yard, London, WC2H 9DP; Telephone 020 7379 7222; Mail order 0161 831 7875; E-mail mail@ nealsyardremedies.com; Website www.nealsyardremedies.com
Neal's Yard has other branches in London and the UK, and selected chemists stock their products. They manufacture and sell natural cosmetics, herbs, essential oils and homeopathic remedies.

Pure Scents
13 Dogpole, Shrewsbury, Shropshire, SY1 1EN; Telephone
01743 356677
This small family-run business makes the most natural and
wholesome health and beauty products. To get the full
benefits on my section on stress relief you should try their
geranium and rosewood bath oil. They have a mail-order
service, so no matter where you live they are never far away.

Natural healthcare and therapies
If you want to find a therapist near where you live or check
the safety/use of a product, these organisations should be able
to help you.

British Acupuncture Council
63 Jeddo Road, London, W12 9HQ; Telephone 020 8735 0400;
Fax 020 8735 0404; E-mail info@acupuncture.org.uk; Website
www.acupuncture.org.uk

British Allergy Foundation
Deepdene House, 30 Bellegrove Road, Welling, Kent, DA16 3PY;
Telephone 020 8303 8583; E-mail info@allergyfoundation.com;
Website www.allergyfoundation.com

British College of Naturopathy and Osteopathy
Lief House, 3 Sumpter Close, 120–22 Finchley Road, London,
NW3 5HR; Telephone 020 7435 6464; Fax 020 7431 3630;
E-mail (the Principal) am@bcno.ac.uk; Website: www.bcno.ac.uk

British Homeopathic Association
27A Devonshire Street, London, W1N 1RJ; Telephone 020 7566
7800; Fax 020 7486 2957; E-mail info@trusthomeopathy.org;
Website www.nhsconfed.net/bha

You can visit the website for a list of hospitals offering homeopathy on the NHS.

The International Federation of Aromatherapists (IFA)
182 Chiswick High Road, London, W4 1PP; Telephone 020 8742 2605; E-mail i.f.a@lcZ4.net; Website www.int-fed-aromatherapy.co.uk

National Institute of Medical Herbalists
56 Longbrook Street, Exeter, Devon, EX1 6AH; Telephone 01392 426022; Fax 01392 498963; E-mail nimh@ukexeter.freeserve.co.uk; Website www.btinternet.com/–nimh

Miscellaneous

Raven
17 Melton Fields, Brickyard Lane, North Ferriby, East Yorkshire, HU4 3HE; Telephone 01482 632512

This is a small mail-order company which stocks all of the weird and wonderful things I mention in the book, including crystals, herbs, oils and jewellery. I use them all the time and the owners, Chris and Graham, have a friendly approach if you need any help.

Sally Morningstar
PO Box 2633, Radstock, Bath, BA3 5XR
Sally sells magical crafts by mail order; she also works to commission, making special pieces for rituals.

Witches Moon
12 Gray Close, Innsworth, Gloucestershire, GL3 1EE
Suppliers of annual lunar charts.

Organic foods and herbs online and by mail-order

I eat organic food whenever I can to keep my body free of toxins. You can try shopping from one of the companies listed below if it's difficult for you to find organic food.

Jekka's Herb Farm

Rose Cottage, Shellards Lane, Alveston, Bristol, BS35 3SY; Telephone 01454 418878; Fax 01454 411988; E-mail farm@jekkasherb.demon.co.uk; Website www.jekkasherb.demon.co.uk

Jekka McVicar grows and sells a huge range of herbs, wild flowers and vegetables. The company is registered with the Soil Association.

The Organic Marketplace

Website www.organicmarketplace.co.uk

This is an online directory of UK organic businesses and products.

The Organic Shop (Online) Limited

Central Chambers, London Road, Alderley Edge, SK9 7DZ; Telephone 0845 674 4000; Fax 0845 674 1000; E-mail info@theorganicshop.co.uk; Website www.theorganicshop.co.uk

An all-round supermarket offering organic fruit and vegetables, meat and dairy products, groceries and drink.

Organics Direct

Leighton Court, Lower Eggleton, Ledbury, Herefordshire, HR8 2UN; Telephone 01531 640826; Fax 01531 640818; E-mail Louise@organicsdirect.co.uk; Website www.organicsdirect.co.uk

This company sells organic foods, vegetables and dairy products.

Piatkus Books

If you have enjoyed reading this book, you may be interested in other titles published by Piatkus. These include:

Art of Sexual Magic, The: How to use sexual energy to transform your life Margot Anand

Balancing Your Chakras: How to balance your seven energy centres for health and wellbeing Sonia Choquette

Barefoot Doctor's Handbook for Heroes: A spiritual guide to fame and fortune Barefoot Doctor

Barefoot Doctor's Handbook for the Urban Warrior: A spiritual survival guide Barefoot Doctor

Book of Shadows: A modern witch reveals the wisdom of witchcraft and the power of the goddess Phyllis Curott

Care of the Soul: How to add depth and meaning to your everyday life Thomas Moore

Chakras: A new approach to healing your life Ruth White

Channelling for Everyone: A safe, step-by-step guide to developing your intuition and psychic abilities Tony Neate

Channelling: What it is and how to do it Lita de Alberdi

Chinese Face and Hand Reading Joanne O'Brien

Clear Your Clutter With Feng Shui Karen Kingston

Colour Healing Manual: The complete colour therapy programme Pauline Wills

Colour Your Life: Discover your true personality through colour reflection reading Howard and Dorothy Sun

Complete Book of Aliens and Abductions, The Jenny Randles

Complete Book of UFOs, The: Fifty years of alien contacts and encounters Peter Hough and Jenny Randles

Complete Book of Women's Wisdom, The Cassandra Eason

Complete Guide to Divination, The: How to use the most popular methods of fortune-telling Cassandra Eason

Complete Guide to Magic and Ritual: How to use natural energies to heal your life Cassandra Eason

Complete Guide to Psychic Development, A: Over 35 ways to tap into your psychic potential Cassandra Eason

Colours of the Soul: Transform your life through colour therapy June McLeod

Creating Sacred Space With Feng Shui Karen Kingston

Dolphin Healing: The extraordinary power and magic of dolphins to heal and transform our lives Horace Dobbs

Encyclopedia of Magic and Ancient Wisdom: The essential guide to myth, magic and the supernatural Cassandra Eason

Energy Medicine: How to use your body's energies for optimum health and vitality Donna Eden with David Feinstein

Feng Shui Astrology: Using 9 star ki to achieve harmony and happiness in your life Jon Sandifer

Feng Shui Journey: Achieving health and happiness through your mind, spirit and environment Jon Sandifer

Finding Fulfilment: Eight steps to achieving your ultimate potential Liz Simpson

Healer Within, The: How to awaken and develop your healing potential David Furlong

Healers and Healing: Amazing cases from the world's best known healers Roy Stemman

Healing Power of Light, The: A guide to the healing and transformational powers of light Primrose Cooper

How Meditation Heals: A practical guide to the power of meditation to heal common ailments and emotional problems Eric Harrison

I Ching *or* Book of Changes, The: A guide to life's turning points Brian Browne Walker

Jonathan Cainer's Guide to the Zodiac Jonathan Cainer

Karma and Reincarnation: A comprehensive, practical and inspirational guide Ruth White

Karma and Reincarnation: The key to spiritual evolution and enlightenment Dr Hiroshi Motoyama

Lao Tzu's Tao Te Ching Timothy Freke

Life After Death and the World Beyond: Investigating heaven and the spiritual dimension Jenny Randles and Peter Hough

Life on The Other Side: A psychic's tour of the afterlife Sylvia Browne

Light Up Your Life: And discover your true purpose and potential Diana Cooper

Living Magically: A new vision of reality Gill Edwards

Many Lives, Many Masters: The true story of a prominent psychiatrist, his young patient and the past-life therapy that changed both of their lives Dr Brian L. Weiss

Meditation Plan, The: 21 keys to your inner potential Richard Lawrence

Mindfulness Meditation For Everyday Life Jon Kabat-Zinn

Natural Healing: Practical ways to find wellbeing and inspiration Chrissie Wildwood

Nostradamus in the 21st Century Peter Lemesurier

Nostradamus: The final reckoning Peter Lemesurier

One Last Time: A psychic medium speaks to those we have loved and lost John Edward

Only Love Is Real: A story of soulmates reunited Dr Brian Weiss

Other Side and Back, The: A psychic's guide to our world and beyond Sylvia Browne

Paranormal Source Book, The: The comprehensive guide to strange phenomena worldwide Jenny Randles

Past Lives, Future Healing Sylvia Browne

Past Lives, Present Dreams: How to use reincarnation for personal growth Denise Linn

Peter Underwood's Guide to Ghosts and Haunted Places Peter Underwood

Pocketful of Dreams: The mysterious world of dreams revealed Denise Linn

Positive Living Vera Peiffer

Power of Gems and Crystals, The: How they can transform your life Soozi Holbeche

Power of Inner Peace, The Diana Cooper

Psychic Pathway: A 12-week programme for developing your psychic gifts Sonia Choquette

Psychic Protection: Creating positive energies for people and places William Bloom

Psychic World of Derek Acorah, The: Discover how to develop your hidden powers Derek Acorah with John Sutton

Pure Bliss: The art of living in Soft Time Gill Edwards

Purpose of Your Life Experiential Guide, The: A practical and intuitive guide to discovering your life's path Carol Adrienne

Reaching to Heaven: Living a spiritual life in a physical world James Van Praagh

Rebirthing and Breathwork: A powerful technique for personal transformation Catherine Dowling

Reincarnation: Amazing true cases from around the world Roy Stemman

Saved by the Light: The true story of a man who died twice and the profound revelations he received Dannion Brinkley with Paul Perry

Scole Experiment, The: Scientific evidence for life after death Grant and Jane Solomon in association with the Scole experimental group

Soul Purpose: Every woman's guide to spiritual growth and personal empowerment Jackee Holder

Sound Healing: Using the healing power of the human voice to heal yourself and others Shirlie Roden

Stepping into the Magic: A new approach to everyday life Gill Edwards

Talking to Heaven: A medium's message of life after death James Van Praagh

Tarot Made Easy Nancy Garen

Teach Yourself to Meditate: Over 20 simple exercises for peace, health and clarity of mind Eric Harrison

Thoughts That Harm, Thoughts That Heal: Overcoming common ailments through the power of your mind Keith Mason

Three Minute Meditator, The: 30 simple ways to relax and unwind David Harp with Nina Feldman

Time for Transformation, A: How to awaken to your soul's purpose and claim your power Diana Cooper

Transform Your Life: A step-by-step programme for change Diana Cooper

Vibrational Medicine for the 21st Century: A complete guide to energy healing and spiritual transformation Richard Gerber MD

Way of Harmony, The: How to find true abundance in your life Jim Dreaver

Woman's Spiritual Journey, A: Finding the feminine path to fulfilment Joan Borysenko

Woman's Magic: Rituals, meditations and magical ways to enrich your life Sue Bowes

Working with Angels, Fairies and Nature Spirits William Bloom

Working with Guides and Angels Ruth White

Working with Your Chakras: An introduction to the energy centres of your body Ruth White

World Mythology: The illustrated guide Dr Roy Willis

Yesterday's Children: The extraordinary search for my past-life family Jenny Cockell

Yin & Yang: Understanding the Chinese philosophy of opposites and how to apply it to your everyday life Martin Palmer

Your Body Speaks Your Mind: Understand how your thoughts and emotions affect your health Debbie Shapiro

Your Healing Power: A comprehensive guide to channelling your healing abilities Jack Angelo

Your Heart's Desire: Using the language of manifestation to create the life you really want Sonia Choquette

Your Mind's Eye: How to heal yourself and release your potential through creative visualisation Rachel Charles

Your Psychic Power: And how to develop it Carl Rider

Your Spiritual Journey: A guide to the river of life Ruth White